GOOD FENCES

GOOD FENCES

The Boundaries of Hospitality

Caroline Westerhoff

MOREHOUSE PUBLISHING
A Continuum imprint
HARRISBURG • LONDON • NEW YORK

First published in 1999 by Cowley Publications, 28 Temple Place, Boston, Massachusetts 02111.

Published in 2004 by Morehouse Publishing, P.O. Box 1321, Harrisburg, PA 17105

Morehouse Publishing, The Tower Building, 11 York Road, London SE1 7NX

Morehouse Publishing is a Continuum imprint.

The Questions for Discussion were written by John Westerhoff

Cover art: "Church and Fence" © Pat O'Hara/Corbis

Cover design by Laurie Klein Westhafer

Library of Congress Cataloging-in-Publication Data

Westerhoff, Caroline A., 1940-
    Good fences : the boundaries of hospitality / Caroline A. Westerhoff ; with questions for discussion by John Westerhoff.
        p. cm.
    Originally published: Cambridge, Mass. : Cowley Publications, c1999.
    ISBN: 0-8192-2140-6
    1. Christian life—Anglican authors. 2. Hospitality—Religious aspects—Anglican Communion. I. Title.

BV4647.H67W47 2004
248.4—dc22

                                                                                    2004044911

Printed in the United States of America

04 05 06 07 08 09   10 9 8 7 6 5 4 3 2 1

For
Benjamin
David and Jonathan
and always
John

Contents

Acknowledgments

Many people have participated in the writing of this book, and I am grateful both to those I can name and to those many others who took part in classes, seminars, and conversations as it was taking shape. They generously fed me with ideas and thoughtfully challenged me with questions.

I thank Bishop Frank K. Allan and the people of the Episcopal Diocese of Atlanta for granting me a sabbatical summer in 1996, starting me on my way. I am grateful to the Trappist Monastery of the Holy Spirit for welcoming me into their community of hospitality as I began.

I am especially indebted to my family, friends, and colleagues for telling me their stories and trusting that I would represent them with care. I am sure it is hard to live and work with someone who is always scratching notes on slips of paper. *What is she writing down now?* While I admit to a bit of artistic license here and there, I hope they are pleased with their contributions.

I credit as representatives of all the people with whom I bounced ideas back and forth the adult classes at St. Luke's, St. Anne's, and Holy Innocents' parishes in Atlanta, as well as summer continuing education students at Columbia Presbyterian Seminary in Decatur, for helping me stay honest and on the mark. From their lively engagement with the material, I experienced anew the learning that comes only from teaching.

Cynthia Shattuck, the director of Cowley Publications and the book's hands-on editor, was once again indispensable to the outcome. She encouraged and chided me, made the focusing and sometimes frustrating query, and just stayed with me all along the way—sense of humor intact. In her devotion to the art and science of book writing—and her care of authors—she is simply the best.

Vicki Black, Cowley's managing editor, added her fine touches to the editorial process—as she gave birth to a son! Her elegant artistic sense is evidenced in the overall design of the book and in the selection of the artwork for the cover. She makes all of Cowley's authors look good.

Finally, my inexpressible love and gratitude go to my best friend, John Westerhoff, for continuing support far surpassing any definition of husbandly duty—especially during the long process of revisions, when certain writers take to loud vocal expression. His confidence in me was always contagious, providing the spark to keep me plugging along when energy waned. His solid and creative thinking aided me in maneuvering around several difficult corners and produced the study questions at the end of the chapters. And thank goodness the man can cook!

My heartfelt appreciation to you all.

Foreword

After the completion of *Calling: A Song for the Baptized*, two of its concepts—boundary and hospitality—continued to play around in my head. I call this phenomenon the blinking neon light effect, and I pay attention when it persists over time.

A boundary is that which defines and gives identity to all types of systems, including persons and communities. Boundaries are both tangible and intangible. They involve physical borders and property lines, as well as names and stories, traditions and values. Without a boundary, whether property line or story line or skin, we do not have anything to which we can point or to which we can give a name. To say it another way, unless we draw a line—a boundary—and say that something lies outside its domain, then we can speak about nothing that lies inside with real meaning.

Hospitality has to do with welcome, with greeting another and extending an invitation to come inside and enjoy each other's company, at least for a while. When I discovered that the words "hospitality" and "hostile" are related to each other, I realized that authentic hospitality must also include welcoming the "enemy" as guest—defining the enemy as anything that is strange to us or perhaps makes us uncomfortable, someone we would like to go away and leave us alone. Indeed, the receiving of all sorts and conditions of men, women, children—and all sorts of ideas and notions—does seem central to the church's mission of reconciliation.

In the midst of these musings, I began to see that the church, in our desire to call ourselves inclusive, is in danger of blurring our boundaries, of erasing aspects of our core identity. And the same can be said about us as persons. In our desire to be accepting, to be too many things to too many people, we can lose sight of that for which we stand—of who in truth we are. Conversely, if we make our boundaries too tight and too restrictive, we run the risk of leaving out something that is essential or enriching.

Boundaries and hospitality go together: they are in a necessary but irresolvable tension with each other. Without boundaries, there will be no system into which anyone could be invited; without hospitality, the system will dry up, will turn in on itself and die. So with this book, I intend to look at the dynamic tension between the two from a variety of perspectives—personal and communal—and to invite readers to work toward their own understandings of the paradoxical twists it introduces. I am not trying to solve a problem—particularly one for which there is no solution. After all is said and done, the question for us as persons and as communities will still remain: *How do we stay faithful to the essence of who we are, holding on to our continuity with the past, and at the same time, welcome the other into our midst—particularly the strange and disquieting other—so that we can change and grow?* We will never finally answer this question; new manifestations will continually pop up. Nevertheless, life in its fullness demands that we persist in facing and confronting the dilemmas it presents.

I see *Good Fences* as a book that will be helpful to church leaders, both lay and ordained, and to dioceses and congregations as we struggle with this requisite tension, as we work to make sound decisions in an increasingly complex and even unfriendly society. Family units will find it useful as well. Maintaining the dynamic relationship between core identity and welcome becomes a task of some urgency as we attempt to respond to the day's pressing concerns in ways that are reflective of God's grace and God's will. A friend describes *Good Fences* as "similar to a theological novel, comprised of short stories woven together with commentary." With this combination of anecdote and exposition, the book provides a framework within which to examine what is at stake as we grapple with the gospel and with questions of diversity—personal, racial, ethnic, cultural, sexual, socioeconomic, and religious.

Good Fences lends itself to group study by vestries and church boards, in classes and reading groups. I hope the down-to-earth anecdotal material will render it both approachable and appealing for personal reading and study. A number of people have told me how the stories in *Calling* served in turn to evoke their own. This was particularly significant in group settings, as members found themselves engaging each other at ever-deepening levels. I expect the same to hold true with *Good Fences*. The questions at the end of each chapter should prove helpful toward that end.

Finally, the book begins with one of those special pieces that just seem to write themselves. I have entitled the prologue "Lines," and while it is not altogether autobiographical, it does chronicle some of my earliest experiences with boundary and hospitality. Please join me as I begin to explore the consequential tension between them.

Caroline A. Westerhoff
September, 1998

Lines

Lines were an important part of childhood—particularly the lines of our games. They taught indelible lessons of ordering and limit, of consequence and decorum; lessons of success and failure; lessons about the way things were then and the way they would later be.

We drew our hopscotch patterns with chalk on the sidewalk or on the broader expanse of driveway concrete. Success meant jumping through those lines without landing in forbidden territory. Sidewalk cracks were another matter. They presented grave hazard—stepping on them broke backs! It was important to take seriously the different lines of childhood.

The bounds of the kickball field were outlined in the hard-packed dirt of the school playground. Success here meant kicking the ball hard and straight enough to carry you all the way around the bases. A weak or off-line kick meant you were out—but even more embarrassing was a clean miss, when your foot made no contact at all and every eye in the place was on you.

I remember the lines that marked the beginning and end of races. In between, you were to run as fast as your pounding chest and flailing limbs allowed. And even long after the footrace has become but a dim memory for most of us, phrases like "toeing the line" and "on your mark" prompt us to take deep breaths and shake out our limbs. They foretell challenges of thought, word, or deed.

Red Rover called your name and dared you to crash through that formidable chain of bodies and linked arms or else be captured and held. Red Rover left bruises on both body and ego of skinny little girls—and skinny little boys too, I suppose. But Red Rover was alluring. Its lines gave us exhilarating tastes of force and might—the addictive rush that can come from imposing your will upon another.

Fortunately, there were lines that taught us about other kinds of power. They carried us beyond ordinary limits and spirited us into realms of imagination and fantasy. Chief among these were the story lines of the adventure games we played, always begun with the incantation "Let's pretend...." Even the least among us could claim heroic endowments simply by uttering the magical words, "Today I will be... *Superman!... Wonder Woman!*" and then tying the requisite towel-turned-cape around their necks. And kite lines rippling above park and beach still mesmerize me, ever steering my vision up into cloud and sky—lifting my eyes from the ground.

The lines in which we moved from room to room and activity to activity kept us in regimental order. Sometimes we were arranged according to height; sometimes, in alphabetical order. Because I was tall for my age, I could find myself toward the end of the line. Because my last name was Askew, I could be right at the beginning. This was good training, as later circumstances in my life bounced me back and forth as well.

Classroom subjects—even the earliest ones—introduced us to their own decorum of lines. I soon learned that color was to be placed within their bounds if artwork was to be hung on the wall. Stray swipes indicated a lack of sense or care. I also learned that elephants always were to be gray, never pink or purple. Sky was blue; grass, green; dogs were often black. Creativity was less prized than conformity. It was important to be right.

I recall the lined pages we painstakingly filled with stylized letters as we labored to master the art of penmanship. These drills never came easy to me, but the fact that we lived in three different cities when I was in the third grade just made the wearisome worse—I was subjected to three very different methods. My hand today remains an odd mix of techniques—lines at some odds with each other.

I remember faithfully memorizing the lines of geography, lines that kept one country, one people, separated from another. It seemed artificial then, and feels even more so now, when many of these learned lines have been eliminated and different configurations have appeared in their stead—new lines to be learned. The lines of geometry were a different matter. They were rubbed out right then. My successive efforts to form faultless circles and angles only left holes in the paper, spots scrubbed raw by my eraser—akin to later spots on my heart, rubbed raw in my efforts to make up for more serious sins of omission and commission.

There were also the family lines drawn to declare limit and bound. I think of the invisible but inviolable one marking the exact middle of the car's back seat. My brother and I were warned that infringement of this barrier by even a finger or a toe would bring down the direst of consequences—usually unnamed—on the perpetrator. Years afterward, I would draw the same line and give the same threat to my young sons—*You will be really sorry if you budge!* Sanity and safety can depend on the maintenance of sturdy lines.

The limit of our circular block was another of these family lines. I was not allowed to cross the street alone, and my first try at running away from home became the frustrating and humiliating exercise of trudging round and round its circumference, small suitcase in hand, until I finally gave out. On this occasion, the umbilical line to sanctuary held. Only after my smooth portrait of childhood became filled in with lines of thought and shadow, would I have the courage to make other decisions, to go farther afield. Subsequent forays from home would involve different kinds of danger—primarily those of association and relationship—and I would come up against those binding words of tradition: "*We* don't do that; *we* don't go there." I would risk incurring the disapproval of generations.

Some of the most rigidly drawn lines that I remember were those of race and class. Black children may have whooped and hollered through the Saturday matinee right along with the white kids in the rural South of my childhood memory, but we did not sit together. They were sent to the balcony above us. At the time I did notice that they sat higher up than we did, but only later would I—with some irony—attach this observation to a phrase about the last being first. They also stood in different lines in front of different bathrooms and different water fountains. Even in those days, I wondered why we took so much trouble.

Class lines were just as fixed but were more subtle—invisible until you ran into them. I did so with my first crush. The subject was a sweet, blonde boy with a soft voice and a gentle smile. I do not remember his name. I sat with him at the Saturday matinee. He was the right color. We did not touch at all, but it was nice to feel him that close. Later, I learned that his friendship was unsuitable. We were far from wealthy, but my grandparents did own the land on which they worked and lived; his family were sharecroppers. The delicate label for him was "common." Something within me still cringes when I hear the word.

I think the first time I consciously defied these lines of social barrier was as a young teenager in suburban New York. I took my stand—drew my line—and refused to swim in the pool of a country club that denied membership to a respected family in our community, members of our Presbyterian church. Their offense was a trace of Jewish blood in the family line. What I failed to perceive in my adolescent zeal for justice was that belonging to this club was a badge of self-worth to my Depression-scarred father. His daughter's refusal to accept the fruit of his efforts was a source of pain to him. Looking back, it has become a source of pain to me—but only after parenthood and age began drawing their softening lines upon my face and my spirit. My ethics may have been sound; my character formation had a way to go. I am sorry that Daddy is dead now and I cannot tell him how I understand. For the present, a line separates us.

Every time we make a decision we draw a line. Indeed, the word "decide" is from the Latin *decidere*, which means to cut off, to follow one line of a fork and not the other. Deciding is like coming to a place on the trail as we hike through the woods, where we have to choose to go this way or that—to take one path at the expense of the other. We cannot travel down both—at least not at the same time. If we are lucky and observant, there are markers to point us in the direction we should take.

The Ten Commandments might be thought of as trail markers. They are there to point us in the right direction, to tell us which line of the fork to follow. They are lines laid down to tell us how we should decide: lines that urge us to put God above everything and everyone, to revere life and respect the dignity of others, and not to long for and take what belongs to someone else. Good and helpful lines for God's people.

A woman who decided wrongly—who chose the wrong fork—is brought to Jesus. She has been caught in the act of adultery. Her accusers—those who decide on behalf of the law—constrain her to stand before him. Jesus stoops and draws lines in the dirt. Then he says to her presenters, "Let anyone among you who is without sin be the first to throw a stone at her." He stoops back down and draws more lines. They go away, and Jesus tells the woman not to sin again. Drawing lines is not a simple matter.

Inside and Outside

*Boundaries are lines that afford definition, identity, and
protection—for persons, families, institutions, nations.
They can be tangible, like the walls of a room; intangible,
like the bonds that encircle a family or a community; or
they can defy ordinary description altogether. A boundary gives us something to which we can point and ascribe
a name. Without a boundary, we have nothing to which
we can invite or welcome anyone else.*

It was my year for a sabbatical leave, and I decided to
begin with a three-day silent retreat at a monastery. I
had never done anything like that before: a solitary ven-
ture of extended silence in the domain of God. The idea to
head off into some kind of self-imposed wilderness was
one of those inspirations that seemingly come out of the
blue. It just struck me as the way to begin what I hoped
would be three months of creative thinking and writing. I
know I was anxious about backing out, because I saw fit
to declare my intention right away to anyone and everyone who showed the slightest interest in my summer
plans. How could I later admit to all those people that the
retreat never happened, that I had been such a wimp? Yet
the prospect of sitting with God for three days—and especially for three nights—gave me cause for dread.

Suppose God were to say things I did not want to hear?
Or worse, suppose God said nothing at all? Suppose the
silence went both ways?

I chose the Abbey of Our Lady of the Holy Spirit, a
Roman Catholic religious house, for my retreat. It
seemed like the right place. I think I was very tired, and
what appealed to me first and foremost was its conven-
ience. This time, I did not want to struggle to the airport
and get on a plane and fly far away. This time, I did not
want to drive in my car for even two or three hours. This
time, I just wanted to arrive, enter, and begin as simply as
possible.

Located about thirty-five miles from where I live and
work, the monastery offered a soothing modicum of familiarity to me. I had been there on a few occasions over
the years for a variety of meetings and remembered the
lovely grounds that provide opportunity for walking and
peaceful lakeside sitting. I knew that the stark, white
stone church would offer a steady setting for periodic
prayer and worship with the monks. Still, this is not to
say that all my memories of the place were good ones. I
remembered making a degrading trek back into town to a
motel bed, before women could stay the night in the retreat house. But that was a long time ago, and the bro-
chure now makes it plain that women and men of
different religious backgrounds are welcome as guests.
Nonetheless, I knew the monastery would afford me a
measure of dissonance. I, the welcome guest, would be
stepping into a religious tradition with which I was not in
communion—although we hold many of the essentials in
common. I would be leaving home, crossing into another
country of sorts. It would be important to guard against
becoming too comfortable and taking too much for
granted. I would need to stay alert, to seek direction from
the landmarks around me.

I turned left off Georgia Highway 212 on a still June afternoon and immediately caught my breath in pure delight. The avenue leading to the monastery is lined on either side by a majestic column of stately magnolia trees. In full flower, their huge, white blooms filled the air with a heavy, sweet, and soothing fragrance that to me, surely flowed straight from the portals of heaven. I curved around to the left again at the sign indicating the way to the retreat house, parked my car, picked up my bag, entered through a glass door, and presented myself at an office window marked "Guestmaster." The narcotic effect of the magnolias had worn off by now, and I felt the familiar tightening of the gut that strangeness and lack of confidence always bring.

The monk inside the small office, dressed in his black and white Trappist habit, did not did not look up from his deskwork. On the window's ledge was an envelope containing a key for room number 202—wherever that was. Clipped to the envelope was a registration slip bearing my name. The brief instructions on a printed card displayed on the ledge asked me to provide an address and a telephone number, put the slip in the envelope, and place the envelope in a small basket. Ever so eager to get it right—to honor the code of this strange land—I carefully did as I was directed and waited. The monk still did not look up. "Is that all?" I whispered. He at last acknowledged my presence, gave me a fleeting smile, and nodded toward an adjacent hallway. I set off in search of my room.

Paying attention to the signs on doors was critical, and I soon discovered that they gave me the directions I needed: "Second Floor," "Women's Toilet," "Women's Shower Room," "To the Church," "Silent Area," "Please Do Not Enter—Cloistered Area." I found my room easily and turned the key in the lock. It was sparsely furnished but pleasant in its simplicity. On the small desk was a single sheet of information telling me where I could go and giving me the schedule for meals and the times of prayer to which I was invited. It was obvious that I was responsible for taking care of myself. A graciously worded paragraph reminded me that while I was welcome to attend daily community masses, as a non-Roman Catholic I could not receive communion; prayer for the unity of the church would be appropriate. Fair enough. I began to feel more at ease—welcomed but more aware of the boundaries.

I spent the rest of the time that afternoon—before vespers at 5:30—getting used to my surroundings. I found it difficult to sit still while I made this transition between home and monastery, so I prowled the buildings and the grounds, always being careful to mind the explicit directions on various doors and fences: "Please Do Not Enter—Cloistered Area." The small bulletin board in the dining room was an additional source of useful information. "If you desire the assistance of the Retreat Director, please leave a note in the frame of his door on the first floor." It struck me that someone who could not read or could not see would have a difficult time making her way around here, and I wondered if the monks ever took that into consideration. I then thought about communities of which I am a member—my parish church, the condominium association, our family. Do we give clear and adequate guidance regarding our expectations of the visitor and the outsider, as my hosts were providing for me? Do we let them know what they are free to do and what is off bounds? Or are we selective in the ways we offer them such information?

I remember only two moments of real consternation for me, both on the first full day of my retreat. I was still trying to learn the ropes, keenly aware that I was not at home. The monastery day begins with vigils in the church at 4 a.m. Not a morning person, I set my clock for

3:30 and hoped for the best. Personal preparations at that hour do not take very long, and I presented myself at the heavy interior door connecting the retreat house with the church on the early side of the appointed hour. I pulled it open and slipped into the dark church. It was empty, and my gut predictably tightened. Where was everybody? Maybe I had the wrong time or the wrong place?...I stepped back into the dimly lighted hallway on the other side of the entrance. "How silly," I chided myself; "there's nowhere else to go!" Thoroughly dousing myself with holy water, I heaved the door open again and reentered. My eyes adjusted to the gloom, and I made my way down the side aisle, rubber-soled shoes squishing loudly on the stone floor. I was relieved to see one monk now in his stall, head outlined in the glow of his reading light. I made my way to the pews assigned to visitors and those on retreat and sat down. One by one, the others began to emerge from the shadows and take their places in the stalls. Little lights blinked on as they opened their books and arranged their music. I took some comfort in noticing that several looked a bit disheveled—not morning people either! The following day at the same time, I encountered another guest hesitating before the same door. He was a sleepy-looking man with a worried expression on his face. "It's awfully dark in there," he whispered. I nodded confidently and waved him in, feeling like an old pro.

The other moment of dismay occurred right after lunch. One of the notices on the bulletin board told me that the rosary would be prayed every afternoon at 1 p.m. in the Guadalupe Chapel. The directions to its location were simple enough. I decided, with some misgivings, that I would join the suppliants in this practice so unfamiliar to me. I arrived at another heavy door about ten minutes early, again the only visible soul around. The posted sign led to the second episode of panic: "PLEASE

DO NOT ENTER—THIS IS A CLOISTERED AREA." Below was a message in much smaller letters, inviting visitors to proceed to the chapel on the left for the rosary. Nevertheless, sheer size told me I should obey the first directive. I walked back down the hall to check the announcement on the bulletin board. Nothing ambiguous here, and back I went to that imposing door. Only a minute or two had passed, and I was still quite alone in the hallway. I strolled around again and then confronted the door for the third time. Sucking in my breath, I lugged it open and stepped into a dark and dank basement-like space. I turned left and entered the tiny Guadalupe Chapel through its curtained entrance. I sat before a large and comforting painting of the Virgin Mary until my companions in prayer—five in all—arrived and began their measured cadences. It seemed quite all right that I had no beads of my own and was obviously following along. While my Mariology may not have been entirely consistent with theirs, I hoped they recognized me as a respectful believer in the communion of saints. I joined them again the next afternoon.

I think I made only one really obvious blunder. I did not realize that the church's side aisle closest to the cloister was for the monks alone. Some of the oldest ones spent many hours there in prayer all day and night. I had been walking around the nave and had stopped to sit for a time to meditate upon the bronze altar crucifix. The guestmaster—I knew him now as Father Anthony—slipped in to inform me gently of my error and invite me to take a chair on the opposite side. No problem. I thanked him, and he slipped away as unobtrusively as he had entered.

The retreat was wonderful—all that I had hoped it would be, and more. In the end, only one of us was silent. In the chanting of the monks and the reading of the Word and the silence of the garden, God spoke clearly. Or perhaps I should say that in my silence, I could hear what I suspect God is saying to me all along. I decided it would become my custom to return to the monastery regularly—to continue crossing the border into that strange but compatible land. Departing was not difficult: checking out was simply the reverse of checking in. I placed my key and the donation for my stay in the designated slot next to the ledge of the office window at the entrance, loaded my car, and drove back around the lake and down through the sentinel magnolias. I glanced at my watch. It was just about time to start praying the rosary in the Guadalupe Chapel.

—Defining Boundaries—

One of the things my visit to the monastery stirred up in me was my long fascination with the whole business of boundaries. This interest is grounded in years of work with church systems and is heavily influenced by my prior training as a biologist. In my earlier book, *Calling,* I defined a living system—whether a community or an organism—as two or more living parts that are related to each other in order to realize a particular aim or purpose. Over time, it has become apparent to me that the characteristic of living systems about which I have the most to say is that of boundary—of the system's being bounded, contained, determined, limited. I have come to realize that this notion of boundary is complex and one that we ignore to the peril of our valued relationships. I further believe that the concept of boundary, put in a theological framework, can give us guideposts for faithful participation in God's reign—our present home and our final end.

A boundary is a line drawn; it is a line that defines and establishes identity. All that is within the circumscription of that line makes up a whole—an entity. Neither "good" nor "bad" in its own right, a boundary determines something that can be pointed to and named: a person, a family, a geographical region, a city, a town, a nation, a parish church, a denomination, a faith. A boundary provides essential limit, for what is not limited—bounded— blends into its context and ceases to exist in its own particular way.

Some boundaries can be seen or touched; others cannot. Among the former are the lines determined and set down by surveyors or the paved streets encircling plots of city land or the dusty roads outlining field and pasture. The border is the line between country and country, and we call ourselves citizens of either one side or the other. The doors and fences marking the monastery's cloister were lines I could reach out and feel, even though I was not to pass through them. I can run my fingers along the rough brick walls of my house and the smooth ones that distinguish my room. These are bounds I have set myself and about which I have some say. The walls of a cell mark the boundary of a prison. The jailed inhabitant has little or nothing to say about them.

My family moved frequently in my earlier childhood years. My father worked for a large corporation for which promotion always meant relocation, and he did well. Even though I was born in Atlanta and have lived here for the whole of my adult life, when someone asks me to name my hometown, I hesitate and then usually respond, "I really don't have one; we lived in a lot of different places." Nevertheless, I am aware that I identify all of those places as home. I still can picture particular houses on particular plots of land located on streets with particular names. I can call them up in my mind's eye. Like the turtle's shell, their walls provided the skin within which our family took up residence for however long we lived in that community. These walls—household boundaries—held the familiar furniture and provided the backdrop for family pictures; they contained the hubbub and the aromas of family gatherings. They offered us a feeling of security and a measure of permanence. I think one of the reasons we were able to maintain our sense of family through all those moves was that we could live within boundaries that enabled us to know and to name who we were. The boundaries of our neighborhoods, the churches we chose, and the schools my brother and I attended contributed as well. In this light, it occurs to me that another perspective from which to reckon the tragedy of the homeless is that of boundaries: these men, women, and children have no stabilizing walls against which they can lean for the identity and security so critical for personal and family dignity.

The horizon is the ultimate line that we can see though never touch. It is always out in front of us, a symbol of future hope and expectation. The horizon is God's line—a divine border, if you will—drawn by divine fingers to distinguish between sea and sky, earth and heaven. I have long thought it the place where miracles are born. I stare at the horizon for hours when I am at the seaside, trying to sort things out and regain perspective, to take back into myself some sense of God's order of things, God's limits. And I recently learned that the horizon is where one fixes one's eyes in order to counter the dizzying effects of seasickness—not a surprising remedy at all! I lose the horizon in the city, where I spend most of my days. It is blocked out by all the buildings and pavement we throw up around ourselves in the rush to achieve and to possess. When life begins to get too jumbled up for me, I know it is time to return to the sea and find the horizon again.

--Boundaries and Story--

There are other lines—a second category of boundaries—that we perceive differently because they are invisible. Time provides us with a good example. While we can measure time by means of watch or clock or calendar—*This appointment will last one hour; I have three weeks to finish the project; if I can just hold on until tomorrow; where has time gone?*—we cannot see or touch it. The boundary of time is invisible but very real and potent. Our acknowledgment and thoughtful management of it enhances our credibility; our cavalier disregard of time causes us to lose the trust and confidence of others.

These invisible lines tend to bind the whole person—head and heart—in powerful ways. They are the cords encircling those who share certain beliefs, understandings, and values or who have agreed to abide by the same rules, regulations, and guidelines. But although they are unseen, we can express these bounds in words; we can name them, talk about them, write about them. Such a boundary is the Benedictine Rule—the rule of community prayer, engagement with the Word, and manual labor, all apart from the world—by which my friends the Trappist monks order their lives. They are the bands encircling family and church; wrapped around team, political party, military unit, around gang or cult. *This is who we are; this is what we do and don't do.* They are the bonds of patriotism and school pride, as well as the lines of racism and classism I encountered as that young child in the rural South. And while we cannot literally see the cord tying together all who have been baptized into the death and resurrection of Jesus Christ, it is implicit in Paul's assertion of one Lord, one faith, one baptism.

The way that these spoken and written lines take on shape and power is often through stories. It has been suggested that the ultimate definition of humankind lies in our ability and our longing to tell and listen to stories, which is something children seem to know without being told. When they ask again and again to hear the story—whatever the story and however many times they have heard it—children are really asking us to tell them who they are, to remind them of the fundamental definitions that give meaning and shape to their lives and their values. *Tell me the story of how you met. Did you love each other from the very first? Tell me about the day I was born and how the sun was shining. Tell me how I got my name. Tell me about when I went to camp for the first time and how I cried and cried—and then cried again when it was time to come home. Tell me about the time you went all by yourself to put Inky, our sick, black puppy, to sleep and then came home and told me and held me tight and this time, shed tears with me. And what about the time I got lost and finally found my way home? You were angry that I left without permission and yet relieved all at the same time. Tell me what you meant when you would say, "I don't care what everyone else is doing. That's just not who we are; that's not what we do!"*

We pass on stories from generation to generation to shape and form character, to pass on the godly and moral code. I always remember one in particular, told at my expense. It recalls the only time in my life when I deliberately stole anything. I was about four years old, and we lived in a sterile, brick apartment complex right outside Washington, D. C., where my father was stationed during the Second World War. My playmate on this fateful morning had received a singular treasure in the mail from his grandmother: a large pack of brightly colored construction paper. Wonderful hues for which I did not yet have names were represented in that amazing stack. We cut and pasted and colored, and altogether too soon, it was time for me to return home for lunch and a nap. I could not bear to leave behind anything as entrancing as that paper, so I took a few sheets of red and blue and green and yellow—and especially some of the marvelous nameless ones—and hid them underneath my coat. My larceny was discovered by my mother only minutes after I removed my wrap. Back on it went. I made my abject way to the neighbors' front door, rang the bell, stammered my confession, apologized and returned the paper, and fled down the concrete steps. I have been embarrassed on many occasions since, but this one remains close to the top of my list of personal humiliations. The rules by which our family lived were made clear for me that day. Inviolable and lasting bounds were set, and they are remembered in each retelling of the story: *This is who we are, and that is not our way.* We do not take what belongs to someone else. My own boys know it well, and I suspect their children will too.

The act of storytelling sets boundaries that speak volumes about safety and consistency, even when the story itself is lacking in substance. Any parent who has tried to cut short the bedtime ritual and been stopped cold in the process can attest to this. I remember being required to read aloud, for seemingly endless months, a little book about three silly ducks that I had unwittingly bought in the grocery store—every word of every line of every page without fail! It was the necessary prelude to restful and interrupted sleep for my young son David. In thinking back on that nightly observance, I now know that its purpose was to assure him of safety and consistency and things upon which he could count.

And there are those stories with all the substance in the world, the ones upon which we not only can count but also are ultimately to better our lives. At the family observance of the Jewish Passover, the *Seder,* the great story of the Exodus is told once again for all to hear. As part of the ceremony, the youngest child asks four questions: *On all other nights, we eat either leavened or unleavened bread; why, on this night, only unleavened bread?* We left Egypt so quickly that our bread did not have time to rise. *On all other nights, we eat all kinds of herbs; why, on this night, bitter herbs especially?* They are reminders of the suffering we endured as slaves in Egypt. *On all other nights, we do not dip our herbs even once; why, on this night, do we dip them twice?* We dip them once for tears of sorrow and once for a sign of hope. *On all other nights, we may sit at the table either erect or reclining; why, on this night, do we recline?* We dine with special ceremony tonight to remember struggle and to celebrate freedom. Every year, the head of the household then retells that foundational narrative of the Jewish people—and of those who share their heritage. From Deuteronomy:

> When your children ask you in time to come, "What is the meaning of the decrees and the statutes and the ordinances that the LORD our God has commanded you?" then you shall say to your children, "We were Pharaoh's slaves in Egypt, but the LORD brought us out of Egypt with a mighty hand. The LORD displayed before our eyes great and awesome signs and wonders against Egypt, against Pharaoh and all his household. He brought us out from there in order to bring us in, to give us the land that he promised on oath to our ancestors. Then the LORD commanded us to observe all these statutes, to fear the LORD our God, for our lasting good, so as to keep us alive, as is now the case. If we diligently observe this entire commandment before the LORD our God, as he has commanded us, we will be in the right."

For us Christians, every time we celebrate the Eucharist together we are remembering our foundational story and taking it into ourselves anew: "Christ has died; Christ has risen; Christ will come again." We tell that story again and again, as we repeat the cycle of the seasons and bring to life those heroes and heroines, scoundrels and cowards who are our ancestors, as we recall both the ordinary events and miracles of their lives—and of ours. Pray that the children continue to ask their questions. The words to an old hymn of my own childhood come to mind: "I love to tell the story of unseen things above; of Jesus and his glory, of Jesus and his love." I am grateful I heard it so many times. It helped remind me of which story to cling to when as a young new mother, things did not turn out quite as I had expected. Those notes are still within me. They help even now.

-Boundaries of Spirit-

Stories also have the power to shape and to form congregations—and thus their members. We have long observed that churches born as the result of conflict and schism tend to live out their conflictual heritage far into the future, repeating cycle after cycle of wrangling and fighting. These patterns are difficult to break because they are the essence of the foundational story. The constant reliving of this story serves to reinforce the congregation's reason for being—albeit perverse—and to keep it alive. Ironically, it is with the open telling and understanding of their history that members have a chance of breaking its hold on them and allowing a new spirit to emerge. A longtime friend reminded me that every church—regardless of its origins—should take the time and trouble to tell its tales, with all the expected ups and downs that go along with living.

Kathleen, a vigorous woman probably in her late sixties, has belonged to the same Episcopal church in a small town in northwest Georgia her entire life. However, the roots of her story in that place go far deeper. Her grandparents became members of the little congregation around the turn of the century, baptizing and raising their children in its midst. Kathleen's own four daughters were baptized and confirmed within its walls; three were married there. Originally built in a field in a residential part of town, the modest gray frame building is historic. It now sits on the corner of an east-west highway, and the neighborhood has changed. A gas station, a school, and an empty lot have taken the place of the homes. The church's flock has waxed and waned and waxed again over the years, and clergy have come and gone, some better suited to the job than others. The members have fought and loved, as those who know each other well will do, but it has long been obvious even to outsiders like me that they have cast their lots in that place and with each other.

One day, Kathleen and I were musing together about history and its power to interpret what is happening today, as well as to give instruction and hope for the tomorrows lying ahead. We cautioned each other about the foolishness of allowing generations to die out without passing on their stories to us, and I wondered what I had not heard from my grandmother's lips because I had not taken time to listen. Then somewhat sheepishly, Kathleen began describing something she does on a regular basis. "You may think it odd and a waste of my time," she said, "but I frequently go alone to the old church and just sit. I'm not really praying. It's more like I'm soaking it all in, filling myself up with its spirit: the smell of the wood, the light filtering in through the windows, the colors, the feel of the carved altar rail—every bit of it. I love being with the building itself, but it goes further than that for me." Kathleen explained that when she is there, she experiences herself surrounded and embraced by all who have gone before; she feels washed over—inside and out—by their spirits. She continued with a wry grin, "As you know, I'm someone with strong opinions, and sometimes I have to find out that I'm wrong!" The old church and the company she finds there, that grand cloud of witnesses, help her do that. They help her regain a sense of peace and purpose. "And," she added, "they also help me grieve."

I assured Kathleen that I did not find her ritual the least bit odd—quite the contrary. Through it she is connecting with the fabric of the old church and joining the communion of those who previously sat where she is sitting. The visible, tangible, measurable walls and pews are doing their part to evoke the invisible and powerful flood of memory and story. Together, they are providing her with a renewed strength of identity, and with a spirit of hope for the future. They are planting within her a re-generated capacity, as she puts it, "to get over the next hurdle." They are reminding her that God still has much to do and would like her to join in the doing.

I belong to a community whose boundary is more difficult to put into words than Kathleen's. I enter it when I take my two-mile walk first thing in the morning, a ritual that gives me fresh energy to get over the hurdles of my upcoming day. The route includes a pine bark trail around a large office park near home. Adjacent to this park is a middle-rise apartment building that provides subsidized housing to older women and men who have immigrated to the United States. A number of them regularly stroll the path, some stopping to sit on the benches interspersed along the way and chat quietly together. I would guess that many come from Eastern European countries, since my Romance-language ear does not pick up the sounds of French or Spanish or Italian—or even of the somewhat familiar German. I feel particularly close to one man, although we have never talked. A stalwart jogger, he flashes a gold-toothed smile and a spirited thumbs-up greeting of both encouragement and triumph every time he passes me.

There are other faces I have come to recognize and who recognize me as well. We nod and wave. They may attempt to say hello in English, while I do a lot of motioning with my hands. I take notice when I have missed seeing someone for several days in a row, and they seem to notice when I have been absent too: huge smiles break out all around when we meet once again. I have come to realize that a mutual spirit of hospitality binds me to these people—a daily confirmation that we are alive together at this time, in this place, and glad to be so. I consider them my neighbors and friends, and I am grateful for our relationship. Our exchanges start my day on its proper course. If asked to describe the essence of this community, the best I can say is that it is marked by greetings repeatedly received and given. I do not know the names of my fellow members or much of anything about them, other than what I manage to piece together and imagine. Since we do not share a common language, extended conversation is impossible. Still, I have come to understand that the connection I have with them is an integral part of my daily rule for mental, physical, and spiritual health. This connection among us seems to be important for a number of them as well. There is a way—albeit elusive—in which we belong to each other.

A boundary of spirit—one that we cannot easily put into words or perhaps do not even want to put into words—is what ties me to my early-morning community. By the way, there is a sad footnote to this story. I probably need to go back and change its tense from present to past, but I just have not brought myself to do so yet. My jogging buddy recently flagged me down with bad news, delivered in broken English: "We have gotten letter—at our building—cannot come here—do not want us!" "Who doesn't want you?" I managed. "Boss of park—wrote letter—to my building—no more—not even on benches!" I am sure the management of the office park is concerned about lawsuits in the event someone falls and is hurt, but my Eastern European neighbor did not understand this. He was puzzled and angry. "Maybe Americans only welcome," he muttered. I shook my head in feeble protest as he walked on back toward the street. In truth, the management probably does not want me there either. I am only one person, however, and they do not know where to find me. Nevertheless, the boundary of my little community has been broken. There are no more smiles and greetings. I have not yet decided what I can or should do. I wonder what it says about me as I wait and do nothing.

Some boundaries then are visible and tangible, some can be portrayed in word and story, while some are lines of spirit, often revealed in ways transcending our ordinary means of expression—a third category, especially recognized by poet, artist, and mystic. Such are the cords of passion binding lover to beloved—"Like gold to ayery thinnesse beate"—passion that erupts in the orgasm of sexual intimacy.[1]

Such is the ring God wraps around the whole created order, the band best realized through sign and symbol: rainbow and dove, cloud and fire, water and wind, bread and wine. This is the ultimate boundary, approached through the deep and wondering eyes of intuition, dream, and prayer. It bursts forth in poem and symphony, on the canvas of the painter, and in the visions of the mystic ones—those holy sightings in which the line separating earth and heaven becomes less definite and more blurred. It shines through the jeweled colors of stained glass windows and grazes the heights of cathedral vaults in musical tones so achingly clear we almost cannot bear to hear them.

–Professing Differences–

A boundary can be likened to our skin. It separates and differentiates what is inside from what is out. It highlights the differences among us. My younger son Jonathan and I are both known for our quick-flaring but

---

1. John Donne, "A Valediction Forbidding Mourning," stanza 6.

short-lived tempers. We are two Aries—birthdays four days apart—if you put any stock in that sort of thing. Our growing up together has been tempestuous to say the least. Fortunately, we communicate well and apologize often. One particular incident often told at my expense has made its way into those annals of family history. Jonathan and I were in the kitchen and had exchanged hot words over some issue neither of us can remember now. In exasperation, I picked up an empty aluminum cat food bowl and slung it at him. My aim was predictably wild. I missed by a mile, and the bowl clattered harmlessly on the floor. I was embarrassed—probably more by my failure than by my action. "Mom," he laughed, "you throw like a girl!" It was not a compliment. "I guess I do; I am one," was my sarcastic statement of the obvious. In retrospect, it was a better answer than I realized at the time. The muscles and bones of my shoulders are not put together like a man's. I cannot give you the precise anatomical analysis, but the effect is that I will never be able to hurl an object with the same force of trajectory as can a male of comparable athletic talent. Indeed, I throw like a girl.

There are other differences among us—those of size and skin tone, sex and sexual orientation, age and intellect, language and culture, interest and personality—differences that are plainly visible, as well as those that only become apparent when we brave engaging each other deeply and over time. I think God delights in our differences and the rich creation our variety and idiosyncrasy provide. How bleak it would be to look around and see only duplicates of ourselves. Such an existence could surely be described as hell.

Paul's words to the Galatians might seem to contradict this. He writes, "There is no longer Jew or Greek, there is no longer slave or free, there is no longer male and female; for all of you are one in Christ Jesus" (3:28).

But we would be wrong to think Paul is simply ignoring the truth and beauty of our peculiarities with these words. He is not saying that our differences make no difference in the ways we see and feel and think and speak. His key phrase is "in Christ Jesus." It tells us that Paul is talking about baptism. He is saying that among us, the baptized, the neat compartments do not hold, the old hierarchies should not count. While all people are different from each other in gifts and appearance and experience and all the rest, no one of us is better in the eyes of God. *Different from is not the same as better than.* Each of us, says Paul, is precious beyond measure. Differences in social standing or class or education or financial resources or church membership do not constitute differences in worth or in the right to life and to joy in life. So it follows that if all are to be included in the bounty of God's providence, all are to be included in our family of faith. Anyone and everyone are included at the eucharistic table. Right? No, I think not—or at least it is not that simple. We have to ask what it means to be there: who indeed are we who gather around that table? What makes us different?

I recently heard the story of an old parish that was in some turmoil about its place in the city's ministry to the homeless and displaced. Under criticism from within and without the church and the city, fueled by newspaper leads and editorials, its leadership was trying to figure out what to do. And then came the sermon. It was delivered by one of the associate priests on a Sunday when, unbeknownst to him, a group of homeless men would be paid by a neighborhood entrepreneur to pack the services in protest to the pending sale of a building owned by the parish. Ironically, the new owners intended to use it to house a variety of social services for the very men duped that day into objecting. Isaias preached in his lyrical Spanish accent. You had to strain to catch every word, but doing so was well worth the effort. His message was crystal clear: "We preach Christ Jesus—take it, or leave it!" *This is who we are, my friends; this is what we stand for; this is the one we serve—take it or leave it.* Isaias wisely did not offer ready answers, but he rolled out the prophet Amos' ancient plumb line of justice and righteousness and challenged the congregation to begin examining the boundaries of their parish against its standards. Nevertheless, the boundary value of hospitality still held that morning, as parish leaders went out of their way to extend greetings and warm welcome to the visitors—even though, as several later admitted, anxiety ran high when they first stepped into that sea of protest.

But while we attempt to stand strong in our identity, it is important to acknowledge that our understandings of who we are and what we stand for do mature and change with the passing of time. We can be dead wrong. The church's past positions on racial segregation and women are cases in point. We currently struggle with various issues of sexual orientation, and outcomes remain to be seen. God continues to offer us new and surprising opportunities to amend our ways and modify our boundaries, and we must pray for a continuing willingness to make our confessions of sin and to grow to maturity in Christ. Yet even with this warning against prideful inflexibility in our stands, we must have a rock-solid foundation if we are to be and do with vitality and meaning. We must have something to which we will give our lives if the church is to endure with integrity and perform with courage, if the church is to be at all different from the culture in which it finds itself.

—Welcome and Inclusion—

We talk a lot about inclusion these days in our increasingly pluralistic society. We construct committees and panels and conference faculties with the politically correct assortment of minorities and "those who throw like girls." We include the younger and the older, the married and the single, the richer and the poorer, the gay and the straight, the "normal"—whatever that means—and the mentally or physically challenged. If we are fortunate, we can cover a number of categories with the same person. Then we hold our breath, worrying that we have left out some group or that we will be accused of treating our selections as tokens, as objects of our concerns to be inclusive.

Although well intended, our current words and practices of inclusion too often can reflect sentimental and sloppy thinking. When we say that everyone is included in our family of faith or at the table, I think we are confusing *inclusion* with *welcome*. True, if we are to be the ones whose particular work is the restoration of all people to unity with God and each other and the creation in Christ, then we must welcome all into our company. To welcome is to receive with pleasure, to delight in another's being among us for a time. The Jesus we follow ate with tax collectors and sinners, listened to Samaritan women, showed compassion and forgiveness to so many more. We are to do no less. We are to receive with hospitality all who present themselves at our thresholds. Yet when we state that we welcome others into our particular boundary, we are also saying that for now anyway, they live somewhere else. One individual house—or church or school—is not right for everyone. To claim that a local congregation can be all things to all people is presumptuous at best, but it is a claim into which we too often slide when we are overly anxious about growing and meeting a budget—surviving in some form, any form, without sufficient regard for the ultimate cost to our identity. As my friend Joe is wont to say, "The recipe for ice cream excludes a lot of good stuff, but if we included all of it, we would no longer have ice cream!"

For there to be an inside, there must be an outside. We must have something into which we can invite others before we can extend authentic invitations. We cannot rely on good intentions alone. In this light, inclusion and exclusion paradoxically become opposite sides of the same coin. Neither makes sense without the other. The word "inclusion" comes from the Latin *inclusio*, to shut in or to confine. To include goes beyond a willingness to welcome, to receive. Rather, it means to take in as a member or a part of the whole. If anyone and everyone are too easily included, we are saying in effect that anything goes. We are disclaiming our boundaries. And as our membership is more and more made up of those who will not or cannot confirm some measure of adherence to the core practices and values of the defined community, that community as we have known it will disappear. Without bounds we are nothing; with different bounds we become something else.

Granted, commitment—like conversion—is not a singular happening. Our commitment to a community or a family grows or diminishes over time. We are included at deeper and deeper levels as we live in that community and come to understand what it means to belong to it. But if even initial membership is without qualification, then we stand for little other than being nonsensically "inclusive." If belonging is without obligation and accountability, then we finally have not joined much of anything at all, and any significance that community might have held for us evaporates like mist. This is why the church's requirements and preparation for baptism and confirmation are so important and why the obligations of financial stewardship and participation in worship go far deeper than merely being means to pay the bills and fill the pews.

For there to be any validity to our life together, there must be substance on the inside to which we adhere—beliefs, values, commitments, loyalties, stories that differentiate us from those outside our boundaries. And ironically, it is this differentiating stuff that will attract those we can then welcome to our community, welcome to come inside so perhaps they can later be included. To say it another way, a system—person, family, church, nation—must have some sense of who or what it is and is not before it can take its place among other systems and connect with them. It must have some idea of the lines drawn around it. Yet boundaries are costly. Part of the cost is that we must take hard and long looks at ourselves, continually asking those questions of identity:

— How do we distinguish ourselves from others?

— What are we supposed to be doing?

— What should we leave alone?

— What can be claimed as ours?

— What belongs somewhere else?

— What are legitimate concerns about our rights?

— How might we discount the rights of others?

— Who is welcome?

— Who might not feel so comfortable among us?

— How much flexibility and tolerance do we practice?

— What is the price of belonging here?

— For what would we be willing to die?

— For what do we live?

Those considering affiliation with us must first join us in asking and answering these boundary questions. If they and we do not, we will pay the highest price imaginable: the loss of our identity. Again, if we do not lay claim to who we are, we will be nothing, and inclusion in our number will have no meaning. But just coming up with answers is still not enough. How we do so and what these answers prove to be will determine whether or not our communities and our dreams are those of God, or are the flawed products of something else.

Jesus asks the disciples, "Who do the crowds say that I am?" They give him a number of answers—John the Baptist, Elijah, Jeremiah, or one of the other prophets. Jesus presses on with the ultimate boundary question each and every one of us will have to answer for ourselves: "But who do *you* say that I am?" Peter answers, "The Messiah of God." This is the ground on which we are to stand: Jesus is the One. In Jesus, God came among us to show us at last what counts. In Jesus, God came among us to welcome and then to include. In Jesus, God came among us to reveal the shocking power of love. If we are to come anywhere close to being who we say we are, we must not lose sight of this ultimate assertion: Jesus is our way and our truth and our life. But to profess that Jesus is the Christ finally is not a matter of doctrine and belief, not a matter of verbal assent. We too are to reveal the shocking power of love. We too are to challenge the principalities and powers—particularly when we are the principalities and powers. We too are to be willing to suffer with and for the other, to give away when we think we can give no more. Like Jesus, we are to welcome strangers and sinners into our midst, just as we ourselves have been welcomed.

-TWO-

Welcome

> *Once our boundaries are defined, questions of hospitality arise—questions about the welcoming of any and all to approach our boundaries and perhaps to cross them. This welcome must include a willingness to struggle with people, ideas, and happenings that are strange and intimidating to us. Otherwise, we risk being closed to life's ongoing need for change and rebirth. We risk drying up and dying long before doors are closed or our last breath departs for other realms.*

The previous owners of one of those houses into which we regularly moved in my childhood had painted its front door bright red. I could tell that this particular aspect of our new home's decor did not charm my mother and father, but I loved it. That dazzling red entrance somehow made living in a new town and going to a new school more bearable. I later realized that my parents must have eventually felt its welcome too, for they did not repaint the door. It looked especially welcoming when adorned with the Christmas wreath that year.

Doors present us with varied and complex messages. They can be the heralds of welcome, or of warnings that we would be wise to turn on our heels and walk away. They offer protection from ambush, but they can also keep us locked away, limiting and isolating us. They hold our secrets safe, but they can block reports of good news from beyond our ken. Doors provide opportunity for movement across the boundary—outside, in; inside, out—but such opportunities also make them dangerous. The front door is the receiving point for guests, but it also receives the knock of the uninvited solicitor or the stranger who cannot come in. The back door is the choice of the vagrant seeking an odd job or a handout, yet it also offers special access to the friend who does not need to knock and who knows the key's secret hiding place. Doors are places of vulnerability, where the boundary can be broken and violated, where identity can be forever changed.

An open door communicates welcome extended, permission given, opportunity offered—acceptance, free-dom, trust. "Come in and join me," says the voice on the other side. "We can enjoy each other's company; we have much to learn from one another." The open door will also lead us outside, providing both entrance and then exit when the time comes to leave—when the welcome wears thin or the going gets too rough or we just need a change of scenery. But be careful not to slam it on the way out: you may want to return another day.

In contrast, a closed door connotes lost opportunity, refused access, denied visibility—rejection, restriction, suspicion. But it also grants sanctuary and safety, hallowed space, peace and quiet, the privacy of retreat—a place to shed tears or erupt in gales of laughter without having to explain them to anyone; a place to pinch your cheeks and fix your hair, gathering your composure before it all begins; a place to whisper soft prayers as you look for the courage you will need to face the world again. I remember that my parents' bedroom door was shut tight every Sunday afternoon while they napped; my brother and I were forbidden to knock. Not a bad idea, I later decided—once I understood!

Doors ajar are somewhere in between; they do not present a clear message one way or the other. I prefer to know better where I stand, even if the word is not the one I yearn to hear. Still, my bedroom door cracked ajar was a nightly necessity of childhood for me. The light left burning in the hall outside at least kept the monsters at bay. Maybe a definite answer is not always best.

Then there are the invisible doors, sometimes open and sometimes tightly shut—depending on who you are and what you look like and where you find yourself. These are the heavy doors of manners, tradition, and custom. I suppose all of us have run smack into them at one time or another, when we did not wear a tie or pick up the right spoon or know the words of the song or were at a complete loss for any words at all—or conversely, when everything began to fall into place and we knew we had done nothing to merit such good fortune. These are the doors of status quo and sameness: *We've always done it this way. Why should we bother to change now?* They also can be the doors of insidious privilege, prejudice, and fear: *You really do not fit in. Why would you want to be here in the first place?*

When I look back on certain other doors of my childhood, I remember they evoked a strong mixture of feelings. Many of those same doors continue to call them forth now: fear and anticipation, dread and exhilaration, sinking inadequacy and soaring confidence. Then—and now—my reaction depended on how sure I felt of the ground in front of that door and on what I guessed awaited me on the other side.

Foremost in my memory are the doors of school and church, doors that sometimes bore a strong resemblance. I needed help opening these exalted doors in the earliest days, help from someone much taller and stronger and—I supposed—thus much wiser than I. They frequently were constructed of heavy metal or thick wood panels, with great handles placed well beyond my tiptoed reach. They conveyed the clear message that something of absolute importance went on behind them and anyone who dared approach better be worthy of admission. I did not intend to be found lacking, and this resolve gave me a stomachache on some occasions: times of examination, recital, and pageant, particularly when I had lines to remember and notes to sing.

Such doors even today can give me pause—I did forget some lines, and the notes were not always on pitch. I still hesitate before them and find myself wondering if it is all right to go in. I catch my breath and pray that no one hears the childish pounding of my heart. But I also realize that I am the taller, older, supposedly wiser one now, and I find myself wanting to throw those doors open as widely and noisily as I can for those who have gathered on the steps beside me. Filled with their own mixture of apprehension and hope, they await entrance, and the treasure inside is far too precious to be hoarded.

Color has always made a difference to me, and too many of those formidable school and church doors were institutional gray or listless brown or worst of all, torpid green—I think it should be a sin to spoil the bright green of growth and new life! Such doors do not invite either approach or entry. If we are to be serious about our welcomes, perhaps we should consider painting all our doors bright red or royal purple or blazing yellow or peacock blue—or springtime green. I had not thought of it before, but the front doors of both my home and my parish church are deep, dark red. *Nice.*

When I think back on other kinds of doors of my childhood, screened ones come next to mind. Lighter in weight than the sturdy "real" house doors, they clattered shut with a staccato bounce—apparently a more pleasing sound to younger than to older ears. Screen doors are marvelously versatile, granting access to breeze, birdcall, and fragrance, while providing a boundary of protection against the marauding mosquitoes of my Southern clime. They let you be inside and outside at the same time. A space equipped with both screen door and ceiling fan has to be what rooms in the heavenly mansion are like.

Akin to screened doors are glass doors and those with windows. They give you a chance to view the world, while affording shelter from the assaults of winter's chill or summer's heat. They permit the illumination of sun and moon and streetlamp to flow into nook and cranny—particularly welcome if the day is dark. They allow you to look outside or in before you risk crossing the threshold yourself—or before you open that door to another. I have always liked seeing where I am heading—and "Do not let just anyone in while I am gone" was forever the rule at our house. I think screen and glass should be required elements in all our different habitations—even though they can render us more vulnerable to the hurled rock or the slung brick. Like drawing lines, safety is not a simple matter either.

In the gospels, Jesus says quite a bit about doors. He talks about open and closed doors and about how we pray. He tells us that we are to go to our room and shut the door before we offer our prayers. Public performance serves as its own reward. Sounds fair enough. Besides, I have always found it hard to listen to anyone else—especially God—when I am concentrating on the appearance I am making. Then Jesus instructs us to knock—to ask, to search—so the door can be opened for us. When we pray, it is helpful to remember there is someone on the other side just waiting to hear, just waiting to come in and sit with us, just waiting to extend a hand of welcome to whatever waits outside.

Jesus says that narrow doors and gates offer the only sure and safe entrance into God's realm of life. Gates that swing too wide and doors that open too fast do not give us the opportunity to slow down and decide what is important before we make our choices. Jesus even calls himself the gate. It is through him that we pass with safety and assurance through all the other doors we encounter. We will have already gone through the one that matters.

—Welcoming Strangers—

A favorite pastime of mine is what I call word digging. It is carried out with dictionary and thesaurus rather than with pick and shovel, but I am sure you get the general idea. On one occasion of indulging myself in its surprises and delights, I made a significant find: the Latin words from which we get "hospitality" and "hostile" are related to each other. Indeed, *hospes* can mean host, guest, or stranger, and the related *hostis,* enemy or host. A trip to the encyclopedia told me that the early hospitals were set up for sick and weary travelers, as well as the poor, blind, and crippled. Often run by religious orders and disregarded by doctors, hospitals long continued to care for persons too poor or too sick to remain at home.

One Sunday soon after my discovery, I was moving rapidly up the sidewalk, on my way from the train station to church. I was running late as usual, having undertaken one-too-many household tasks before I shut the front door and set out. A man and a woman were walking toward me—not too clean, not too dirty. They were homeless; I could tell by the bundles they carried, probably everything they owned. Other than noticing her unnaturally red hair and large, gold hoop earrings, I gave them scant thought. But as the man moved on by me, the woman stopped as if to speak. "I'm sorry; I can't give you anything," I said, beating her to the first word. I thought she wanted money, and I had none. I do not carry much when I am on the city streets; I figure it is safer that way.

"I'm not asking for money," was her snappish rejoinder, delivered with a toss of the red hair and a jangle of the earrings. "No," she continued, "I have a message for Atlanta: if you really want to help people like us, you need a drop-in facility—a daytime place where we can go to the bathroom, take a shower, and wash our clothes." She explained that some of them are just passing through, and they need places to rest and to clean up—like they find in other cities. "If you want to be a really great one, you're going to have to be more welcoming. That's my message for Atlanta. Now make sure somebody hears it!" I nodded obediently, not exactly sure whom I would tell. Still, the woman had reinforced my newly formed definition of hospitality: welcoming the stranger, perhaps even the enemy, as guest.

Indeed, the relationship between the words "hospitality" and "hostile" helped shift my thinking away from any sentimentality I might have about "easy" hospitality: warm invitations, gracious gatherings, extended hands, friendly faces, ample food and drink—whether these be at wine and cheese gatherings in our homes, church coffee hours, parish suppers, or celebrations of the Holy Eucharist. I grew increasingly sure that our responsibility to be hospitable—to invite and to welcome—goes far beyond neat and clean occasions of familiarity and comfort. Like it or not, I had to begin expanding my limited definition of hospitality—and by the way, my equally restricted understanding of evangelism. Both now must include the stranger and the enemy—the ones with whom I am uneasy and who, if I am honest, I would just as soon not have around.

Strangers are not just those people I do not yet know. Strangers must include those I have no *intention* of knowing, for all kinds of reasons that I deem sound and good.

In the same way, strange ideas are not just those with which I am unfamiliar. They should also include the ideas that inspire fear in me, the ones that will disturb my settled notions and even cause me to change my mind. The enemy is anyone or anything that upsets the status quo—endings, beginnings, birth, death. The enemy can be people who are younger or older than I, those who remind me of what I can no longer be and of what I am well on my way to becoming. Sometimes the enemy is whatever alters the way things are, the way I have ordained they will be. The enemy is anyone who asks perverse questions and who disrupts and demands, who threatens to wrest control—illusory or not—from my hands.

When looked at in this way, the *enemy* can begin to take on the connotation of *friend*. Without such enemies in my life, I run a great risk of missing out on so much rich color and variety and spice. I run the risk of being dead wrong about too much that matters. And Christians run the same risks when we do not interpret evangelism as the welcoming of all those fascinating and terrifying sorts and conditions waiting at our doors—evangelism that has as much to do with our own transformation as with changing the lives of others.

Benjamin Britten bases his cantata *Rejoice in the Lamb* on a long poem of the same name, written by the eighteenth-century poet Christopher Smart while he was in an insane asylum. Smart was deeply religious but had a strange and unbalanced mind. Although chaotic in form, his *Rejoice in the Lamb* evidences frequent flashes of genius. Its main theme—and that of Britten's cantata—is the worship of God by all created beings and things, each in its own way. In the fifth section, Smart uses the mouse as an example of a creature's praising God by being just what the Creator intended it to be—in this case, hospitable even to the menacing cat:

For the Mouse is a creature of great personal valour. For—this is a true case—Cat takes female mouse—male mouse will not depart, but stands threat'ning and daring.... If you will let her go, I will engage you, as prodigious a creature as you are. For the Mouse is a creature of great personal valour. For the Mouse is of an hospitable disposition.

While not exactly welcoming the presence of his feline enemy, the mouse does not run from it either. He rather stands fast, ready to take on whatever comes his way as a result.

I received a memorable lesson in hospitality when I was in the tenth grade—although standing fast was only at my mother's insistence. Our class advisor, Mr. Stevens, was out for a long period of convalescence that fall. He was a favorite teacher who managed to make Latin and French palatable for even the most undistinguished of language scholars. The substitute who stepped into his shoes would have had a difficult time under any circumstances, but the difference between the two of them appalled us. Mr. Stevens could only be described as the epitome of middle-aged good looks and savoir-faire, a dapper dresser with a wry and sophisticated humor. In contrast, the substitute was a gangly, inarticulate, and bespectacled young man, fresh out of teachers' college, who wore the same shapeless corduroy jacket over his too-short, high-water pants each and every day.

We clever ones quickly addressed the intolerable situation. The seating chart fell into shambles; no one answered to the same name from one day to the next. Mysterious objects—wads of paper and chewing gum, blackboard erasers, pieces of chalk—flew around the room, accompanied by unnatural sounds and the wheezes of suppressed laughter. How proud we were of our efforts on behalf of all that we deemed tasteful and worthy of respect! The future of civilization rested safely in our hands.

Dismayed by the escalating pride and glee in my lengthening nightly supper reports, my mother determined it was high time to take matters in hand herself. She decided to invite the offending young teacher and his wife to our home for Thanksgiving dinner. Adamant that Thanksgiving is a family holiday, I was horrified beyond measure. The day was for us; there were not supposed to be strangers at the table—much less two such unacceptable ones. Having them there would ruin everything—and would destroy my tenth-grade social standing to boot. But my mother turned a deaf ear to all my protestations. She did not budge. They came. They sat at our table. We broke bread together and said the prayers and passed around the favorite family anecdotes, and it was all right. Our guests shyly joined in and seemed to appreciate having a place to be for the holiday.

I did not say too much about the occasion at school, but my reputation did not seem to be affected one way or the other. What did change was the classroom atmosphere. The high jinks abated, and a semblance of order was restored. I would later learn that if you change one part of a system, the entire system becomes different. I think this is what happened here: my perspective was changed—even if just a little bit—and so the group of which I was a part shifted a bit in its tone. The young man turned out to be a decent teacher. He survived, along with the rest of us, until Mr. Stevens' return.

It is funny how the memory of that particular Thanksgiving has remained vivid over the years, especially when I read Jesus' words about who occupies what place at the table, about hospitality to guests from the streets: those who do not look the way they are supposed to look and act the way they are supposed to act; those who will never be able to repay our hospitality and whose names we certainly will not remember; those who will never come again and swell our membership rolls, who will just disappear. Yet we—I—still can be so keen to draw those hard and fast lines that keep us all in the right compartments. We can be so sure about who is to mix with whom, so certain about correct codes of appearance and behavior. Yes, we think civilized values rest safely in our hands even now.

The recollection of that Thanksgiving Day—a eucharistic day—also continues to remind me of something else: the very act of breaking bread with each other sets the stage for reconciliation. As we share the bread that literally feeds our blood and bones, we receive the spirit that nourishes our ties of understanding and appreciation, that breaks down the barriers among strangers. It is not by accident that the primary symbol of our life together is the eucharistic board around which we are to gather and eat in response to God, our ever gracious host. But then God is the host at every table at which we take our places and pass bread and wine—and milk and soup and holy cheese. It is not by accident that the last occasion the earthly Jesus spent with his disciples was a common meal in which even the betrayer participated—after Jesus washed his feet. Talk about welcoming the enemy.

After his death, two of Jesus' dispirited followers are trudging back along the road to Emmaus. They are rehearsing again and again the events of the last few days, futilely hoping that they can come up with a different ending, a more satisfactory conclusion to his sad story. A mysterious stranger joins them. He tries to interpret for them all that has transpired, to little avail. Arriving in Emmaus, they invite him to stay and eat the evening meal with them. After all, the sun is almost down. He does, and in the breaking of the bread he becomes known to them—their eyes are opened. In this story, a stranger is welcomed as guest to an ordinary meal in an ordinary house with an ordinary loaf of bread. This guest is Jesus—the one who seems to show up when life pushes us right to our limits, when its realities are inescapable—and he becomes the rightful host. The ordinary meal becomes an occasion of conversion for those at his table. That is what we mean by sacrament.

The risen Christ is always ready to take his rightful place as host—to break and bless and give to us. All we have to do is invite him to come through the door and sit down. But if we do, we run the risk of having our eyes opened, of seeing as God intends us to see. That is what we mean by transformation. And being transformed—over and over and over again—means that henceforth nothing will ever be quite the same for us.

—Uninvited Guests—

It is fair to say that sometimes we do not choose to invite; our only choice may lie in struggling to welcome. My coming to receive the intrusion of an uninvited guest with acceptance and then gratitude marks a watershed in my life. The occasion was the birth of my first child—a boy. We named him David, after his paternal grandfather. I would have chosen the name anyway: it means "well beloved."

I had had a little minor spotting early in the pregnancy, but nothing had come of it, and the nine months otherwise went according to expectation. Labor began on a February evening, and we made the mad dash to the hospital—with literally hours to spare. David was born early the next morning. They gave birthing mothers a general anesthetic in those days, and my first conscious stirrings found me alone on a gurney in a hallway outside the delivery room. A nurse and a strange doctor soon made their appearance and began to tell me through the druggy haze that everything was not as it should be. I shook my head in protest, not really understanding what they were trying to say. It seemed to have something to do with the baby's hands. I was taken to my room; my distressed young husband was out making telephone calls to family and friends. Only when he arrived back at the hospital was a nurse willing to bring the baby in to me. By this time, my worst fears had outstripped the actual circumstances, so I did experience a measure of relief. David did not have all of his fingers and toes, and several that he did have were misshapen. His feet were as severely clubbed as they possibly could be, but his head and face were perfect. He was the most gorgeous baby I have seen to this day, and I fell in love with him at first sight.

There were voices in the next days that instilled in me a measure of hope and optimism. Helen, a recent acquaintance, hurried to the hospital with a present for David—a clear plastic ball encasing a bright, rotating butterfly. She told me of her own first child, born with a severely cleft palate. "It's hard to hear now, Caroline, but things are going to be all right. You—and David—are going to be just fine." The young plastic surgeon with frayed cuffs reassured me, saying this beautiful, bright baby could be anything he wanted to be—"except maybe a brain surgeon; however at the moment, I wouldn't even eliminate that." There was the encouragement of a nursery attendant: "Honey, you've got enough milk to feed every baby in there! Don't you let them talk you out of nursing him." I didn't. Nevertheless, most people—including doctors and nurses—in their zeal to say the correct thing to me, seemed to be living in a world of wishful thinking. The obstetrician went so far as to suggest that the fingers might grow back!

For the first time in my twenty-four years, something of absolute importance had not turned out as I thought it should. What I had expected failed to come about. While I would not have put it this way at the time, it had become crystal clear that I was not in control of anything. And furthermore, I was not sure anyone else—meaning God—was either. Everything upon which I had counted was suddenly up for grabs, and it was now my task to welcome this uninvited enemy of pain, confusion, and fear as guest.

Some months after David's birth, I managed to stammer out my dread—and by then my anger—to a wise priest of the church. He listened hard. My fear was that either God did not care or was not around at all, and I cannot say which alternative was more terrifying to me. However, neither one has ever proved to be the case as the divine "enemy" has continued to intrude into my life. Then and later—now—as I have summoned the wherewithal to express my doubts and my displeasure, God hangs in with me, and our relationship moves to new and sturdier places. I have found it works that way with my human connections as well. I also have come to realize in hindsight that some measure of my childhood faith must have remained intact during those dark days. Never for a minute did I believe that the God I was doubting was responsible for David's difficulties—even so David and I could rise above it all and be "better" people. Their unknown cause was certainly not God's doing: inflicting pain and distress—pernicious enemies—is not God's way of achieving divine purposes. And I have long been grateful that such a consequential time of enemy welcoming came so early in my life. It set me on a path that has been rich and vital.

I purposefully chose David's younger brother's name just before his birth three years later. It is Jonathan, and it means "Yahweh has given." Yahweh indeed has given a great deal, including a steadying sign to an anxious young mother. At the precise moment I began to fear for that pregnancy, Jonathan delivered his first strong kick! And after years of casts, surgical procedures, crutches, and occasional stints in wheelchairs, David is the young man the surgeon predicted he would be. An avid cyclist, talented player of several stringed instruments, natural handyman and mechanic, holder of two academic degrees with intention to pursue the vocation of teaching, he is as whole as they come. David never dwelled on there being anything was wrong with him—or maybe he just had it in him from the beginning to welcome his enemies as guests.

And at the other end of life, each of us—including David—will have to come to terms with the enemy death in one way or another. Death is the guest who always lingers at the doors of our lives or perhaps more accurately expressed, the one outside whose door we wait for admittance. A woman I know told me about her Aunt Sally's way of coming to terms with this uninvited guest. Sally was not about to do any welcoming. She had given up on herself and on life in general; she would just take whatever came.

Oh, she could still move around pretty well and could certainly think for herself; but she had had a couple of bad falls, and the family did not consider it safe for her to continue living alone. They selected a nursing home run by an order of Roman Catholic nuns and moved Sally in. She immediately countered by literally taking to her bed. She shunned fellow residents who came to her door to welcome her, turning her back to them and her face to the wall, feigning sleep. She refused to go to the numerous social events sponsored by local churches and civic groups, and she repeatedly claimed to be too sick to make it to the dining room—even and especially in a proffered wheelchair. Fortunately, stubborn Sally met her match in the persons of those equally obstinate nuns. They conferred and came up with a plan—a rather creative one at that: they would thrust reasons to live upon Aunt Sally whether she liked it or not! They asked the family for a list of her special interests, and they chose Lucy—a short, tough, no-nonsense sister—to be their emissary to her bedside.

For starters, Lucy entered the room and informed Sally that God had sent her to the nursing home in order to tend the plants in the solarium, which were dying from neglect. Sally was at a rare loss for words. As far as she knew, she had never received a message straight from the divine lips in her entire life, but she decided this was not the time to question the source of this one. After all, the woman was a nun! Sally got up, put on her robe, and reluctantly made her way to the solarium. She fertilized and watered the plants, pinching off a few dead flowers and moving several to better locations in the sun. She then resolutely returned to her bed. The next morning, Sister Lucy again made her entrance and delivered another pronouncement from God: "I have sent you to this home to supervise the planting of a garden." She interpreted, "God thinks we need fresh flowers for the residents' rooms and vegetables for the table." Lucy thereupon turned on her heel and swished out the door. This time, Sally actually had to get up and get dressed. Organizing her project took most of the day, and she ate and slept better that night than she had in months. Nevertheless, once the garden was staked out and going strong, she increasingly found reasons to remain in her room. Lucy and her sister nuns were again ready with a singularly clever intervention: "God has sent you to this home to play the organ at mass!"

Obstinate Aunt Sally now balked. Even conveyed by a nun, these direct messages from God were getting a bit much. God certainly had better things to do than cajole an old woman at the end of her life. She held out for a few days, until her God-given love of music caught up with her. Then she surreptitiously made her way to the chapel and softly tried a few notes. The sisters—stifling wild cheers of success right outside in the hall—were sharp enough to act as if they were unaware of her movements. Sally sneaked back and forth for a few more days and finally allowed that she would play the organ for them—on occasion.

Here was the really tricky part of the nuns' plan: Sally was a decent musician, and decent musicians do not like to sound bad. Although the actual time involved in playing for a service was modest, she would have to practice, and practice she did. Before long, she was the regular organist for the home. Heaven forbid if anyone else tried to sit down at her instrument! She also became the frequent accompanist for evening songfests around the piano in the dining room. Sally was alive and—given her age—very well. As we might expect, minor skirmishes between her and the nuns continued—with the latter usually prevailing. Still, what with her houseplants, the garden, and her music, she resumed a rich and full life at the home right up until her death several years later. She just needed a little help from some friends in coming to her own terms with an uninvited and unwelcome guest.

In similar vein, my father had a very difficult time with his retirement. Daddy—like too many of us—defined personal worth according to productivity, and his productivity only had to do with the output of his employment. Encouraged to retire early, he lost a sense of purpose when the active days of his career were too quickly over. I will always believe that his illness and death from cancer in his early seventies came on sooner rather than later because he was neither ready nor willing to cross the threshold into free and open time. I believe he chose in some measure the final threshold in its stead. How I wish Daddy had come up against Aunt Sally's nuns! The one who told me stories and who held open so many of those heavy doors could have used help himself with welcoming the enemies for which he was so unprepared. Perhaps the best gift I can give him now is to attend to my own transitions with care and to be accessible to others in theirs—when the time is right for them.

—Mystery and Struggle—

Finally, there are all the welcomings that come between the first and the last. And the older I get, the more I attribute them to God—the one who continually makes my personal "enemy" list, with all those pushings and proddings and beckonings that God seems to favor. How many times have I laughed at myself and sighed, "One more opportunity to stretch and grow—to stop...start over...try again...leave behind...step out...take a chance...change my mind"?

Even so, a favorite story of mine has long been the one of Jacob's wrestling with the angel on the banks of the River Jabbok as he anxiously waits to meet up with his wronged brother, Esau. While Jacob does prevail and receive his blessing, he nevertheless comes away limping and bearing a new name—a new identity. No longer is he *Jacob*, "the supplanter." Now he is *Israel:* "God rules"—God's will be done. Inviting and welcoming the enemy as guest are dangerous undertakings. They always entail the risk, even the certainty, of changed lives. But unless we dare to wrestle with strangers, to receive unexpected and challenging blessings, we hazard lives of deathly sameness. As we choose to hover behind closed doors, we face the consequences of silent thresholds. And do not forget: *We are also the enemy strangers that others are struggling to welcome in their own right.* Stepping over the threshold and through the door ourselves is just the other side of the same coin. What any of us will find there is largely unknown. Mystery must be part of welcome's mix.

I had a recent conversation with a colleague about comprehending the complexities of life. At one point I asked him, "Do you really want to be able to understand everything?" He said, "Yes, I would. I know I can't, but that's different." He admitted, "I honestly would like to be able to solve the riddles, to put the puzzle pieces together, to understand how it all works." And I—a daughter of the sciences—surprised myself by responding, "I did once, but I don't think I want to anymore." As I have mulled over my response since then, I think I was acknowledging that some things are better just *being there* in our midst, making their own profound statement about what is real and true, and the best response I can make is to catch my breath and rub my eyes. Every time I am willing to stand calmly in the face of mystery, knowing that I finally can neither control nor manage it, I know I have realized a small measure of spiritual growth. A God I can figure out is not a God in whom I can have much confidence. A God I can manipulate is not a God whom I should trust.

Still, I was one of those children who constantly strove—not so much to wrestle, but to get the *right* answer. I blush to remember the number of times I hurried forward to the teacher's desk at the end of a class to make sure I had it all down. I must have driven them crazy in my zeal to get it right. On the other hand, I was rewarded with good grades and honors; the system blessed me well for having the right answer so often. Yet I remain grateful today to two teachers who succeeded in thwarting my efforts to know most things beyond the shadow of a doubt, who encouraged me to wonder and to struggle—to invite mystery as a guest. One was a formidable professor of English at Agnes Scott College. I had remained in respectful terror of her my entire freshman year. Then came the paper. I do not remember her assignment or its content, but I will always remember the sole comment she wrote in her precise hand at the top of the first page: "Miss Askew, I do not agree with your position in any way, but you have presented and defended it well." That was it—except for the letter "A."

The other was a mentor with whom I studied in my professional training. Another formidable character, his charge went something like this: "It is my task to tell the truth as I see it." And he did so with force and passion. But he immediately would add, "It is your task to challenge me when you think I am wrong. If we both are faithful to our tasks, *together* we will come closer to approximating the truth." Then he would warn, "But if you do not challenge me, you will destroy our work, and the truth will remain hidden from us both." This same man loved to pop unexpected questions out of left field. I will always remember one in particular: "Is there anything for which you would die?" I answered quickly and predictably, "Yes, of course; I would die for my husband and for my children." He pressed on, "Would you die for the church?" I thought about the institution with all its complexity and failings, the institution with which I can have such a love-hate relationship, and I said, "No." He shook his head. Hastening to please him—to give the right answer—I lamely added, "I would die for Jesus; I would die for what the church represents." "But can you separate them so neatly?" he asked. I told him I would think about it. I still am.

What I learned from these two wise people is that finding the right answer is an intricate task. They taught me that there are always other sides, other dimensions and perspectives to the answers we seek, and we must be hospitable to them—welcome them—if we hope to grasp the larger and truer picture. Indeed, we are to go so far as to search them out, even when such searching threatens to overturn our precious but modest understandings. What finally will destroy persons, families, communities,

and faith traditions is our refusal to receive those who dif-
fer with us about the right answers—those from whom
we are so sure we have nothing to learn.

These teachers also presented me with the priceless
gift of faithful struggle. They sounded the challenge to
wrestle in the company of God and neighbor with the
truth as I perceive it today. I heard from them that we are
always to live in the tension of standing firm for what we
believe and of knowing that we can be—will be—wrong.
Living in this tension between making a statement and
listening for the word we do not yet have is what it takes
to remain alert to God's will for us. It is daunting work. It
requires us to ask our questions not just when we think
we have the answers, but when we are not sure at all,
when we are sticking our toes over into uncharted territory. No wonder we pray at baptism to receive "an inquir-
ing and discerning heart, the courage to will and to
persevere, a spirit to know and to love you, and the gift of
joy and wonder"! Without heart and courage and love
and wonder, we have no hope of welcoming stranger and
enemy—or Friend, at the deep levels of connection that
bring us delight.

Connections

> *Boundaries separate and define us so that we can be to-*
> *gether. If we do not assert who we are and what we are*
> *about—if we try to be everything to everybody—we fi-*
> *nally will have nothing to offer anyone. And if we do not*
> *make the effort to learn who others are and what they are*
> *about, we will not be able to connect with them and re-*
> *ceive all that they hold out to us.*

My friend Maria is a respected Atlanta sculptor and a fine lay theologian. We talk together less frequently than I would like; I always see my own work from a different perspective when we do. Maria is particularly known for her large, three-dimensional installations sited in public spaces. She designs such works to invite both physical and mental participation from those moving through them. Constructed out of recycled airplane parts, *Ex-Static* stands at the corner of West Peachtree and Pine Streets. I come upon it every Sunday morning as I walk from the Civic Center train station to church, and I am pleased that the city retained it after the 1996 Summer Olympics. The points and curves, the huge wheels and wire mesh of *Ex-Static* invariably serve to catch me up anew in the motion and playful activity of the city—not a bad preparation for worship.

Maria has a current exhibition in a local gallery, carried out in collaboration with a composer and a landscape architect to produce a compelling environment of winding paths, red clay soil, bark fragments, and other natural details. She describes *Event Horizon* as "a space that allows people to contact themselves in a deeper way than they usually do." She intends it to allow a response, not dictate one: "I want people to know their deep connections with life by being present in the moment to what is both outside and within them."

Maria goes on to say that a major life theme for her has always been to look for those different perspectives from which to consider all that she does. She even tells of taking aerial photographs of plowed fields dusted with snow as a preliminary step in developing an earlier installation. She lives in a loft apartment, her bedroom high above her studio, and sometimes she finds herself snatching glimpses of what she is doing below. Her present view is of stones and long steel tubes, of large chunks of granite and charcoal studies of rock forms. "From time to time, I find that I just need to step back and look from outside and beyond at what's going on down there. I have to detach myself in order to see the richness that otherwise would be hidden from me," she explains.

My conversations with Maria remind me that there are always different perspectives on either side of every line we draw and every boundary we encounter. We must not assume that everyone looks at that line or sees that boundary in the same way we do. Being in relationship entails seeking out these other viewpoints and comparing them with our own, realizing that without them we cannot hope to envision the whole picture. To put it another way, boundaries define us, even separate us, so that we can be together. They reveal who we are—our identity—so that

we can have relationships of meaning and substance.
Thus in writing of his closest friend and all they meant to
each other, the philosopher Montaigne explained, "It was
because you were you, and because I was I."

-Knowing Who We Are-

The possibility of making connections with one another
increases as we become surer of our own identities. Most
of us have been in a dramatic production at some time in
our lives. We know that the plot assigns different parts to
different actors and that it is essential to stay within their
bounds and limits if the piece is going to work. But suppose those playing Hamlet and Ophelia did not know who
they were to be or what they were to do, when they were
to enter or to exit—stage right or left? The great solilo-
quies would not be heard—or at least not in the right
voice—and madness would be more pervasive than even
the script allows. "Is it my turn to die now, or is it yours?
Are you to kill me, or am I to do you in this time?" If all
the lines were interchangeable and the actors never knew
when they were supposed to speak or to remain silent,
there could be no dependable cues from anyone else on
the stage. A hodgepodge would result, and I doubt any
audience would stay in their seats for long. The paradox
is, only as we recognize the boundaries set by who we are
can we hope to enter into a real relationship with someone else.

Claire and Dan were in my adult education class.
While we were discussing the boundaries and limits that
are essential to our identities, she told a revealing story
about their first or second date. "I must have had a sense
that the relationship was going somewhere, so I blurted
out a question to Dan that surprised even me at the time.
You can laugh, but I had to ask him, 'Do you believe in

God?' He looked a little taken aback, but he answered, 'I guess I must; my father is a Methodist minister.'"

"I was a staunch Roman Catholic at the time," Claire explained, "and I realized I couldn't marry anyone who couldn't make that statement of belief. That was the line I drew for myself even in those early days." Picking up the story, Dan joked, "I know now that my answer about my father really said nothing about who I was, but I'm sure glad she bought it!" The couple later did look for and find a church home within which they both could be comfortable and could raise their children. Still, that basic piece of their identity has held over the years: they consider themselves to be people of God.

Lack of definition about who we are—about our personal and communal limits—presents us with undesirable and destructive ambiguity. Picture a set of paints with each square of paint contained in its own neat compartment. When the colors run together, the result is a muddy and nondescript mix. On the other hand, when the artist applies combinations of paint with intent and care, each color either will maintain its own integrity or will become part of completely new and vibrant ones. In the same way, when I have no boundaries for myself, I will tend to invade yours. When you have none, you will encroach upon mine. Wholesome connections only become possible when two people—or two groups—know who they are and who they are not, what they bring to the relationship and what they do not, what they seek from it and what they might want to avoid. The sure and well-delineated boundaries of the monastery where I went on retreat, for example, helped me see who I was and what I had come to do while there. I have had similar times of self-awareness during foreign travel. The obvious boundaries of unfamiliar language and custom move me to look more closely at myself and my own distinctiveness—how I am both different from and similar to those among whom I am staying—and thus to enjoy my visit even more.

I know a large, no-nonsense black woman who works in a school with children who, for a variety of reasons, do not fit into regular classrooms with ease. Shirley's students frequently have been expelled from other schools, and their normal behavior too often is just plain disruptive. Yells and insults at anyone and everyone within hearing range, along with the loud bumping of desks and chairs in the middle of lessons or study halls, are common occurrences. Arguments occasionally turn physical if teachers are not on their toes. To state the obvious, if they want quiet and submissive respect from their students, this is not the place for them. But if anyone is up to the challenge presented by this school, it is Shirley. Her sense of her own identity—what she will put up with and what she will not—is perhaps the greatest asset she brings into the classroom each day. She believes that her firm and unrelenting grasp of who she is and what she stands for has helped her move into relationship with more than one of her pupils.

When a group of educators in our diocese met one day, Shirley told us about a particular boy, Cliff, who had become the bane of everyone's existence. His mother had no idea how to handle him, and the teachers who passed him along from grade to grade—he read with difficulty—had no clue for her either. The other children either delighted in baiting him until he lashed out at them with profanity certain to get him sent from the room again, or they avoided him altogether. Cliff was a street thug in the making before Shirley resolved otherwise. "While I don't find the word too attractive," she confessed to us, "I 'bullied' him into a relationship with me! Maybe I wanted to show him that he wasn't the only tough kid on the block." Time after time, she literally backed Cliff into a corner, letting him know in no uncertain terms what she expected of him and what the consequences would be if he did not measure up. "We often found ourselves standing toe-to-toe, with me yelling and shouting at him and Cliff yelling right back at me." For a long time, neither one of them blinked. Then Shirley began noticing that their shouting matches were occurring less frequently and that he occasionally mumbled, "How ya doin'?" when he came into her room. He seemed to fit in better with the other students too—which in this school meant that he now got into trouble along with the rest of them and not entirely on his own. Shirley closed her story: "How I have loved this child! I guess that's what finally got through to him."

As I pictured Shirley and Cliff's noisy showdowns, I remembered that fascinating tale in Genesis about the bargaining session between Abraham and God over the fate of Sodom. God joins in—perhaps even enjoys—the lively debate, and Abraham is up to the challenge. He hangs on doggedly, not relenting until he has a satisfactory answer: the city will not be destroyed if ten who are righteous are found within it. With their stories, Shirley and Abraham were reminding me that refusal to engage will destroy a relationship—or prevent a potential one from forming—more quickly and completely than passive indifference, and this includes our relationship with God. God expects us to take up our parts in the give and take between heaven and earth, as well as in the exchanges with each other, even those that are loud and toe-to-toe. The worst thing we can do is turn away from another in cold silence.

I recently had to represent my boss, the bishop, in a meeting with a frustrated and angry diocesan board. Their understanding of the purpose for which they were formed was not the same as his. As a result, they felt unheard and unappreciated, while he wondered why they did not just go ahead and get on with things. I explained the bishop's position that afternoon until I was blue in the face, but I really did not have the necessary authority to answer the board's questions to their satisfaction. I found myself in the unenviable role of scapegoat—the recipient of the brunt of their wrath. Papers were waved in my face, fingers were pointed, voices were raised.

Finally, like Shirley, I had had enough. I surprised even myself when I blurted out my exasperation: "I am very angry. I feel attacked and battered by you. I am not your enemy, and I do not appreciate being treated so rudely. And you haven't even called me by my right name: I'm Caroline, not Carolyn!" I stopped with that. My heart was pounding rapidly. Everyone was quiet for a while—breaths around the table were sucked way in. Then one of the men said, "I'm sorry... Caroline; this has gone too far." He managed a tentative smile at me, and I nodded back. You could see faces soften and shoulders relax. My flare-up had eased the strain we were all experiencing. To the board's credit, they accepted the outburst and put it to good use; things could have moved in a different direction. We decided together that a meeting with the bishop was the next step, and I agreed to set it up. As we rose to leave, we shook hands all around and exchanged a few embraces. The man who had first spoken allowed, "We are a hundred miles farther down the road than we were when we started today." I firmly believe that in declaring myself and my limits—in drawing the line and pronouncing my name—I had helped make connections among us more possible.

–Naming Names–

Our names are part of our personal boundaries, part of our stories. In the ancient world, the name was more than an identifying designation: it connoted the essence or character of the person. The ancient Hebrews indeed shied away from writing out the divine name—one too holy to be used in ordinary ways. When Moses asks God his name, God replies with the mysterious YHWH, a derivation of the verb "to be": *I am what I am; I will be what I will be.* Even Moses is to come no closer. In the biblical story, changes of name mark significant changes in the character or circumstance of the bearer. Abram, once only "exalted ancestor," becomes Abraham, "ancestor of a multitude"—father of all the nations of the earth. Jacob, "he supplants," emerges from his encounter with the angel as Israel, "the one who strives with God"—and prevails. Jesus tells Simon son of Jonah that he is now Peter, the rock on which he will build his church. Saul, the zealous persecutor, comes to be Paul, the great missionary to the Gentiles. In contrast, we know that traders and masters forced African slaves to accept names different from their original ones as a cruel but effective way of molding submissive identities.

Anything but submissive, Marcia, a member of one of our parishes, had a good story about naming for me. She explained that she was raised an Orthodox Jew, but her teacher in Hebrew school would not allow her to become a bat mitzvah until she told the class of thirty students the two Hebrew names that she received from her maternal grandmothers. Marcia refused, turned on her heels, and walked out the door, never to return to the school again. "One of the names is Miriam, but the other rhymes with an anatomical part," she explained. "To reveal it would have set me up for great teasing, and I just couldn't have stood it." Her journey into the Christian faith was long and intentional, but she is sure the incident around her names was one that helped set her on her way. "I guess I just wasn't ready for anyone to know that much about me," Marcia admitted. Then she added with a wicked grin, "And I didn't tell you the name either, did I?"

We Christians acknowledge this power and significance of naming on the occasion of baptism. This is when we receive our given names in the body of Christ and join with everyone else whose surname is "Christian." With baptism, the truth about who we are becomes recognized and said out loud for all to hear: *Do not fear, for I have redeemed you; I have called you by name, you are mine.* Someone has said that it is the task of the church to take us in her arms and rock us and always tell us our names.

My Christian name became Caroline on April 6, 1947, the Sunday I was baptized. The parents of my maternal great-grandmother, natives of South Carolina who were living in Texas for a time, established it in the family line three generations earlier. They named their baby girl Carolina Sumter Smith; I later knew her as Miss Carrie. This name is part of my heritage, my story—my boundary. I hope to be able to pass it on through my sons to a granddaughter or great-granddaughter someday—but who knows about such things? I have had to work hard to claim my name for the better part of six decades. It often comes out "Carolyn" or sometimes "Carol Ann." Both are fine enough; they just do not happen to belong to me. My ears really do not hear Carolyn as much different from Harriet: neither has much connection with the person I am. People who know me fairly well also know that it is a bad sign when I do not correct someone who addresses me by the wrong name, for it is an indication that I have given up and no longer care—or that I do not feel safe enough to do so.

I recently met the father of a six-year-old Caroline at the home of a mutual friend. In a matter-of-fact way, he told me that the child's first-grade teacher had recently announced that she would call her Carolyn, since there are two Carolines in the class. I reacted with stored-up years of frustration: "She can't do that; it's not her name!" He looked chagrined. "No, it's not. I guess it's the teacher's problem and not hers, isn't it?" I nodded vigorously. "I'm glad I met you today, Caroline. My daughter does

have a beautiful name—and it belongs with her," he concluded. "Please help her hang on to it," I urged him. I
wanted to add that like all the rest of us, she will have
enough trouble hanging on to the truth about who she is
and what she stands for in the years to come without her
name being compromised. But I did not know Caroline's
father that well, and the words might have revealed more
about me than I was ready to at the time.

If we do not or cannot assert who we are and what we
are about—or are not heard when we try—finally we will
have nothing to offer any relationship. We will not be
able to extend a meaningful gesture of welcome to friend
or enemy. And if our names and our stories are critical in
defining our identity, both personal and corporate, that
sense of identity only suffers and disintegrates when they
cannot be told or received. To offer hospitality then is to
create safe spaces in which these connections can occur,
places where we will be able to name names.

Bob is the director of a facility where persons—some
of them homeless—with HIV/AIDS can come during the
day for food, conversation, and community. He and his
staff have worked to make Common Ground a setting in
which what he calls a "hearthfire" can burn. "We show
our guests a possibility that they probably haven't had
before: a chance to give a little bit of themselves and to
tell the truth," Bob explained to me. He describes the day
home as a place where they get know each other's first
names. Those who present themselves at the door may
arrive with the survival mentality of taking and grasping
that is so prevalent on the streets. But as they let themselves be accepted and learn to confront each other honestly, they come to find that they have a respected seat at
the table and in the fire's circle. They come to find that
there will always be enough room for them, and they
cross some inner threshold and decide to tell their own
stories—to make an investment in themselves.

"I can only describe this transformation as the reign of God becoming apparent in our midst," Bob went on. He and his staff constantly have to remind themselves that they are not the ones who will build it. In fact, they have to practice a kind of detached connection—to move back a step or two—if they are to recognize what is occurring. "You see, there's a mystery at the heart of it all, and our response in the face of it can only be one of awe and wonder." He closed our conversation with a nice metaphor: "All of us first-name folks—the residents and the regular volunteers and staff—are weaving our individual threads into a common cloth, and the mystery holds it all together."

Chris also talked to me about naming names—in his case, the impossibility of doing so given the number of people he sees every day. He is the director of a large, urban parish's community ministries, and his frustration was running high when we met. "Shoot, *I* don't even know the real names of most of them, and I've been involved here for years!" Chris and the parish leader were in the throes of reassessing a long-established ministry with the homeless. They had earned a citywide reputation for providing simple lunches to longer and longer lines of desperate people—mostly black men. Now that there were additional locations making food and other services available, they were beginning to ask whether their response should be modified, whether they should be about something more than just handing out soup and sandwiches.

Chris laid out for me his belief that the primary cause of chronic homelessness is the lack of significant and supportive relationships for those who still have a grain of hope that their lives could be different. The only thing resembling a relationship that the homeless have is too often with each other—those who are equally without resources. "Their sole connecting link is that they breathe the same air. That's not good enough, is it?"

Chris shook his head, smiled self-consciously at me, and confessed, "Sometimes I look at one of them and think, that's some mother's son—or daughter. And I wonder what hopes she had for him."

Instead of just soup and sandwiches, the members of the parish wanted to provide surroundings in which they could make personal connections with the homeless—an environment in which strangers would no longer remain strangers. Chris continued, "As with anyone else, when you make a personal connection with a man who is homeless, he becomes a real human being to you, someone with his own stories and dreams." But offering such a setting would present another dilemma. The congregation would have to concentrate on helping fewer numbers of people if they wanted to know them and be known in return. Still, they realized that as long as they tried to do too much for too many, they would have nothing of substance to offer anyone, including personal safety. Chris added, "It seems to me that this is how Jesus went about things—focusing on that small group of disciples." He stopped, thinking over what he had just said about Jesus, and then went on to reflect ruefully on the long lines standing out on the street every day. "How can we say we are extending hospitality, when we allow people whose names we don't know to broil or freeze or get soaking wet as they wait for hours to come to the table? And then they have to enter through the back door!" The parish had decisions to make. And as we know, drawing those lines is not a simple matter.

–Making Choices–

My friend Tony decided to leave a rather prestigious job. Her words to me were distressing: "I found I could not work in a place where no one cared enough to know anything about me. Maybe I was looking for an unrealistic and even inappropriate intimacy—but I don't think so." This very sensible and practical woman could find no way to make the kinds of connections she expected and needed, and the situation finally became untenable for her.

The word "intimacy" comes from the Latin *intimare*, to intimate, to make known. Along with the personal things we make known as relationships develop among us, like our names, we are also to make known our expectations—the rules, if you will, by which we are playing. And we are to hold each other accountable for maintaining them. Perhaps Tony could have been more forthcoming about her expectations of her coworkers whom she found unresponsive. She also might have found out something about theirs in return. Shirley's "bullying" of Cliff included the repeated spelling out of her expectations of him: "I love you, and this is what we are going to do" was the consistent message in everything she did and said. In telling the diocesan board that I did not expect to be dealt with rudely, I was holding them accountable for their treatment of me. In like vein, Chris had talked to me about his problem with a sympathetic, open-arms approach with the homeless. He is afraid it too often gives them the message that anything goes and reinforces the very practices—drug use, violent behavior—with which they so desperately need help. With something akin to a mischievous glint in his eye, he asked, "Didn't Jesus challenge and confront, while he welcomed and healed?" And would it be too presumptuous to say that Abraham was holding God accountable to his understanding of who God is when they had their conversation about the fate of Sodom?

With accountability comes choice. We choose whether or not we will play by the rules, whether or not we will stay connected. In our conversation, Bob recalled a time when the hearthfire had gone out at the day home:

"There was a coldness to the place." The survival mentality had taken hold, and stealing and fighting had become commonplace. He and his staff realized that a line had been crossed. They had to reclaim their "sacred space," and so they closed down for a week and went on retreat to look again at their guidelines. Upon return, they made it clear to everyone right up front that they reserved the right to do random drug testing. Bob told me, "We've never resorted to it, but we sure cleaned the place out. People now can choose whether or not to come here based on who they are and who we are, and that's as it should be. After all, doesn't God allow us to choose whether or not we will be part of the Kingdom?"

Over time, God has shown us the divine bounds in a variety of ways to keep and protect us—with the Law, the Beatitudes, and the commandment that is greatest of all: *You shall love the Lord your God with all your heart, and with all your soul, and with all your strength, and with all your mind; and your neighbor as yourself.* These are the divine rules within which we can live life to its fullest measure in connection with all others—if we choose to do so. The baptismal covenant is our assertion of God's boundaries. Every time we reaffirm those promises, we remind ourselves of the expectations God has set for the divine reign. We decide to live within them once again as we agree to teach and learn together, to break bread and to pray; as we say we will resist evil and repent and return when we wander afar; as we vow to proclaim and seek and serve and love wherever we find ourselves; as we pledge to strive for justice and peace and dignity for everyone—with God's help.

Some years ago, the world saw the remarkable scenes of Pope John Paul's meeting with his would-be assassin at Rome's Rebbibia Prison. Whatever desire the pope may have had for retribution, he put it aside in favor of his need to forgive—to acknowledge the God-given kinship between himself and the man who wanted him dead. "I spoke to him as a brother," John Paul declared. No matter what Ali Agca said or did not say that day, the pope was dependent upon something passing between the two of them for his own soul's health. He knew that unless he chose to acknowledge their relationship, he could not be free from the destructive demons of hatred and fear. And we have another paradox—that indicator of truth, according to an early mentor of mine: *Only in connection can we finally find freedom.* The symbolism of the act, captured by a photographer and television crew, could not be missed. John Paul was showing us that relationship and agreement are not the same thing. Being in relation with another entails extending one's hands across boundaries, even those of terror and violence, in spite of anything that has happened—because God wills us to do no less. Because that's the way God puts it all together.

Jesus told a number of parables about choice and relationship—stories we must read with care, for the meaning of a parable is never the most obvious one, but lies underneath the surface. In other words, if we think we have got it, we probably do not. Parables are Jesus' invitation to see how things are in the realm of God. They offer us encouragement to use freely and without coercion the hammer and chisel of our minds and hearts to quarry that truth for ourselves. The purpose of a parable is to subvert our present understandings, to turn our comfortable order on its head. So if we are wise, we will approach a parable on tiptoe—especially one as familiar as that of the prodigal son.

I think this story is among the most misunderstood in scripture, and there are several reasons why. First, we fail to notice its context. The entire fifteenth chapter of Luke's gospel is devoted to stories of being lost: we have the lost sheep, the lost coin, and now the lost son—or sons. In each of these stories, Jesus sets forth God's anguish and then God's boundless joy when what has been lost is restored. The second reason we can miss the point is that the popular title of this parable is misleading: to call it "the prodigal son"—or even "the prodigal father," as some suggest—throws us off the mark. The word "prodigal" means recklessly wasteful or lavishly abundant. While both the younger son's spending and the father's giving can be so described, we fall into error when we focus on any one character of the story. The key line is the first one: "There was a man who had two sons." The story is about all three of them and their relationship.

The younger boy really is not all that bad. He asks for his share of the estate—as the second son he receives one-third. Albeit selfish and shortsighted, such a request was probably not that unusual. The young man goes off to see the world, to make his fortune in distant lands. He does not manage himself or the money very well, and a famine finds him feeding pigs and coveting the very food they are eating. Now feeding swine is just about the lowest state to which a Jew could fall, and having hit bottom, "he comes to himself." What a wonderful phrase: he comes to himself. This is not who I am. These are not my people. This is not my home. The theological word for this is, of course, repentance. It means to turn around, to go in another direction—to become reconnected and hospitable to your true self, to head back where you belong. Frederick Buechner writes:

> To repent is to come to your senses. It is not so much something you do as something that happens. True repentance spends less time looking at the past and saying, "I'm sorry," than to the future and saying, "Wow!"[1]

The younger son turns around and goes home, and he is welcomed by his extravagantly forgiving father. *Wow! I once was lost but now am found, was blind but now I see.*

But remember that Jesus said, "There was a man who had two sons." So the parable does not end here with the younger boy's return and the celebration, but continues with the self-righteous recoil of the older son and his confrontation of the father. *What in blazes is going on? What's with the party and the gifts? He doesn't deserve them after what he's done. I've been here all along doing my duty and working hard. I've been responsible. What about me? He's taking what's rightfully mine, and he isn't entitled to a cent of it. He hasn't earned it. Let him fend for himself. It's only fair.* Our wails of sanctimonious indignation may be loud, but what we deserve has never been God's rationale for handing out extravagant blessings. If this were true, none of us would make the grade; none of us would pass the test. We may go off for a while, but when we return we will find that God has not moved. God is always waiting to receive us with the wide-open arms of the cross. We the baptized could say that the eucharistic feast is the party God throws for us when we find our way home again.

When the older son assails his father with furious protests, he refers to his brother as "this son of yours." He disavows his relationship with his sibling; he breaks the family connection. The father's responding phrase, "this brother of yours," reaffirms the bond between the two sons. He offers the reconciling word, the healing alternative. That is what our work is always to be: opening the door to reconciliation and restoration. But it is important to remember that reconciliation is never cheap or sentimental. It involves telling the truth, and then once the

---

1. Frederick Buechner, *Wishful Thinking: A Theological ABC* (New York: Harper and Row, 1973), 79.

hard word has been said, the slate is wiped clean. The old
has passed away, and everything is once again new. We
can start over; we can move on. That Jesus leaves us
hanging right here is the genius and summons of his
story. We do not know what the older brother does. We
do not know if he brings himself to embrace his family.
We do not know whether he goes to the party or slams
the door on the celebration and takes up an existence of
isolation and alienation. We do not know whether he
chooses to remain lost or allows himself to be found.

I have long struggled with this parable. On the surface, the reason for my difficulty is both simple and predictable: I am a first child—a classic first child, as those
familiar patterns go, ever wanting to please and make
things right for my beginner parents. I was responsible
and conscientious. My bedroom was usually kept in an
orderly fashion, and I moved out of it with little protest
when my grandmother arrived for her annual visit. I fed
and cared for the dogs and cats I adopted. I made good
grades. I returned home at the prescribed hour. My
brother—five and a half years younger—came nowhere
near meeting my standards of rule and responsibility. On
the other hand, my serious bent was no match for roly-
poly Benjy's irrepressible good nature. It was as if he
kissed the Blarney Stone on emerging from the womb.
Never "bad" in any real sense of the word, his ability to
find trouble often equaled my penchant for good behavior, and as we grew older, the comparisons between us
seemed to grow starker. His ordinary grades were rewarded when improved; my above-average ones were
simply expected. His untidy habits became hilarious family anecdotes. Curfews were more lenient; financial assistance, more generous. "It isn't fair," was my frequent
whine before I retreated into my self-righteous shell.

Benjy—now Ben—has joined me in crossing the
fifty-year threshold. Life's turn of events has left its

mellowing marks on us both, and the passing of years has given us permission to make our peace. Ben is a respected husband, father, and grandfather, and I have long since acknowledged my various sins of omission and commission. Although I can still rail against anything I experience as a double standard and self-righteousness can lure me into its poisonous web, remembrance of my youthful grievances has dimmed as time has gone by. I have begun to come to terms with the implications of the parable and its challenge to us to choose connection and relationship over separation and barrenness.

And finally, some measure of understanding and acceptance is essential if we are to decide to be together. An attractive young woman I know recently told me about the loss of a precious relationship—that of her best friend from their growing-up years. "I guess I'm naïve, but I still can't believe what happened," she said. After a long period of self-searching, Howison came to realize that she is gay, and she wanted to tell her old friend Pat the news. She was confident that of all people, Pat would rejoice in her newfound emancipation. Instead, Pat suddenly became increasingly unavailable for their regular lunch and movie dates, and then she stopped returning phone messages left at her office and her apartment altogether. Quite literally, Pat chose to remove herself from Howison's life. It was as if a high, thick wall had gone up between them—one around and over which neither could maneuver. "But I'm still the same person," Howison protested, "still the one she's been with all these years. So I guess we really didn't understand each other that well after all." She had crossed a line she had not even known was there, and she was not so much expressing anger as mourning what she saw as their mutual blindness and loss. She concluded her story with a question: "How could we have seen each other in such narrowly defined ways?"

-Branches of the Vine-

God's intention is for connection among us. As members of God's created order, we have our own identity and particularity, but we also depend on each other—need each other—for fulfillment. None of us has it all. Indeed, the Latin root of "depend" is *dependere*, to hang down from, to rely on. Unfortunately, perhaps as a result of our obsession with self-sufficiency and independence, we have become suspicious of words like "need" and "dependence." Saying that we need another—or even that we need God—is too often named as weakness, not as a basic condition of relationship. To redeem these words, I think we must stop confusing need and want.

Though often used interchangeably, the two words do not mean the same thing. Needs are what we must have to live. To live as God expects, we need community and solitude, stimulation and stillness, feast and fasting, celebration and meditation, hospitality and boundary. These needs reflect our legitimate dependence on God and on each other, and the ability to acknowledge authentic neediness is a definition of humility and of wisdom. In contrast, wants—possessions, status, financial security, physical health, perpetual youth—are what we would like to have to live as we expect, whether or not it is in accordance with God's will. Wants play into our self-centeredness and can destroy our rightful sense of connection to all others. And of course, God knows both our needs and wants long before we are aware of them ourselves. God waits for our response in that conversation between earth and heaven.

In the fifteenth chapter of John's gospel, Jesus gives us help in defining the fundamental relationships God invites us to enter. He does so through an allegory of vine, vinegrower, and branches to teach how things are ordered in God's realm. Beginning with one of the great "I am" statements in scripture, Jesus describes how we are to be together: "I am the true vine. The truth of my life, death, resurrection, and continuing presence is to be your defining bond." His person—and all that he was, did, and is—becomes the central structure that connects everything else. This is why the church is called the body of Christ. This is why we who are members of that body call ourselves one. Without this core reality of Jesus Christ, we have no possibility of knowing the unity that God intends for us and for everyone and everything within creation's bounds.

We the church—lay persons, bishops, priests, and deacons—are the vine's branches. None of us is any better or worthier than the rest, but each has a particular place to be for the completion of the whole. There is no possibility of singular individualism within the baptized community. We live fully as we remain connected to the vine and thus to one another: we are mutually dependent. Things can get difficult and messy for us in these relationships, which are frequently tedious and trying, but we cannot be Christians alone. Jesus tells us that only as we abide in him and in his community—as we stay connected—will we be vigorous, green branches bearing the rich fruits of God's realm: healing, teaching and compassion; generosity, patience, and perseverance; cheerfulness, affection, and all the rest. If we do not stay connected to him and to each other, the needed nourishment of bread and wine and spirit cannot flow to us. We will become dead sticks that dry up and fall away. We will be good for nothing—except fuel for another's fire.

We are now ready to add the third piece of Jesus' allegory. He says, "I am the vine, you are the branches, and my Father is the vinegrower." Jesus describes God as the keeper of the vineyard, the one who knows the essential conditions for health and maturation—conditions of leanness and simplicity that fly in the face of our long lists of wants. God's baptized community of branches will not

flourish and prosper if its accomplishments and acquisi-
tions define its identity more than its life together in love.
Furthermore, the thriving vineyard of God's realm is
never ingrown. It exists for the purpose of feeding others.

Some years ago, I came upon the teachings of the
Grubb Institute of London, England, an organization
founded to study and consult with social systems, including the church. They introduced me to a new understanding of roles, one that continues to offer insight as I think
about connection and dependence, about our being
branches of that holy vine. For the Grubb theorists, the
purpose or aim of a particular system always determines
its roles. They define roles as the various parts that the
system—identified by the lines drawn around it—asks its
members to take up toward the realization of that purpose. Unlike the rather arbitrary and sometimes static
ones into which we step as players in a drama, these roles
are fluid. They move and change as we consider how we
can best carry out the purpose in a given moment, a given
context. In the church, for example, our stated mission is
to restore, to reconcile, and to nourish. Among the roles
we can name—all mutually dependent—are those of pastor, teacher, administrator, worshiper. Because they are
fluid and open to interpretation, we must continually reexamine how we function in them if we are to be diligent
in our pursuit of that mission. Questions we might ask
ourselves include: Is a lighter touch called for here, or do
I need to be altogether serious and forthright? Is this a
time to be directive, or should I take a back seat and let
matters run their course? Do I even need to be there, or
should I stay away? What will foster renewal and reconciliation on *this* occasion in *this* place? Nothing more,
nothing less.

In the instance of a family, the purpose of the system
might be stated as providing encouragement and support
for its members so that they can move into creative and

responsible lives in the larger world. In this light, I recall learning to ride a bicycle and my father's and my roles in that considerable childhood milestone.

The neighborhood in which our family lived that year had no sidewalks, and so it was in a front yard full of large pine trees that I began practicing the elusive art of balancing, pedaling, and steering—all at the same time! My father and I developed a daily ritual. He and I would begin at one end of the yard and move diagonally over the slick bed of needles, taking full advantage of what little open space was available. Daddy would hold the two-wheeler until I was comfortable on the high, black seat, my feet planted on those slippery, spinning pedals and my fists white-knuckled on the blue grips splendidly adorned with red, white, and blue streamers. Then he would walk along beside me—left hand firmly gripping the back of the seat, right hand gingerly maneuvering the wobbling handlebar—until he thought I had enough momentum and balance to continue on my own. Invariably, the end came all too soon, as one of the thick-barked monster trees sucked me in with its bike-attracting magnet. My precious Schwinn—Daddy had bought it secondhand and secretly repainted it in the basement for Christmas—began to show scratches, and so did my skinny arms and legs. I suspect these cuts and scrapes hurt him far worse than they did me, but we both persevered, and I finally celebrated my graduation to the wider and headier world of the neighborhood streets.

Several insights from these early bicycle lessons remain with me. While one might argue that our roles were pretty well spelled out for us, both my father and I stayed true to them. He was to guide, to provide stability and security, to encourage. And he was wise enough to know that he must allow me to do my own work. He never climbed on the bike to show off his own prowess to whoever might be looking on, and he also realized the necessity of his letting go—even when it meant the anguish of a crash. For my part, I was the learner, and unless I had been willing to cooperate with my father and to keep brushing myself off and getting back on that bike, nothing would have happened. Neither of us could have pulled it off in just the way we did without the other.

Nor did I ever see the front yard as the ultimate destination. What a waste that would have been! Rather, it afforded a safe place in which I could be equipped for whatever lay beyond. While it did not shield me from the bumps and bruises that came my way, the yard was protected and predictable enough to allow the work to proceed. Later on, it became the center of my repeated rhythm of moving out and returning. I would set forth to know the agony of pedaling to the top of a steep grade. Then I would realize the abandoned thrill of flying back down, brakes off, wind whipping through my hair. I would return when my expeditions beyond the boundaries of the yard had worn me out and I needed rest and refreshment—renewal for the next day's expedition.

In many ways, this back and forth rhythm to and from my yard suggests to me the weekly movements to and from the altar of my parish. It suggests that the form—the bounds—of the liturgy is what enables me to nourish my connections to the Holy One and thus to be about that mission of reconciliation. So suppose we were to define the purpose of worship distinctly as this: to create an environment in which the worshiper can move into more intimate communion with God. I wonder how such a plain understanding would affect our appreciation of the role of the worshiper and how it might transform the ordering of the Sunday morning event. How long would the sermon be? What would be the nature of choral presentations? How much time would we be willing to leave for silence and meditation if we decided to get out of the way and allow space for God to speak and be heard?

What would happen if we saw worship as the active and essential work of the *people*—the work that enables them to move back out into the world, brimful of the peace and power and presence of Christ; the work that prepares them once again to keep on making connections? Especially the hard ones.

—Holy Ties—

True connections can carry us through times of crisis and transition. Anne's first husband had committed suicide, and she raised their three children alone. She later met and married Ed, a robust man in his early sixties who thrived on strenuous physical exercise and labor. His pride and joy was a lake house he had constructed himself from the ground up, and every spare minute found him out there—hammering and nailing, planting and weeding, cutting and chopping. For her part, Anne took great pleasure in quietly fishing off the dock he had built and putting up vegetables from the garden. But then Ed developed diabetes. He lost one leg and before long, the other. No longer able to work out at the lake, he began to talk of suicide.

As his condition grew steadily worse and the specter of a nursing home began to loom, Ed dwelled more and more on the lake house he would never see again. Sam and another friend from church caught wind of his longings. Somehow they realized the significance of that place in preparing him to get on with whatever lay ahead, and they offered to take him to the lake to spend the night. Ed accepted reluctantly—he said he did not want to be so much trouble to anyone. Everyone, including Ed, knew it would be for the last time.

The two men gingerly negotiated Ed's large frame down the steep incline, and after a supper of freshly caught fish, they sat with him for hours on the porch, listening to the water lapping against the dock. They talked a little about the weather and fishing and the state university's football prospects. At last, Ed got around to the subject of dying. "I'm afraid," he whispered roughly. "I know," Sam replied, "but I have to believe it's going to be all right. Maybe there'll be another lake house where you're going." Ed responded with a chuckle, "Wouldn't that be just fine and dandy?" More lapping water. An occasional fish broke the surface. Then Ed blurted out, "I love you guys. I'm going to miss you." They cried together quietly—perhaps a first all the way around. After a huge breakfast of more fish, they packed up the next morning and went home. Ed was now ready. He had a stroke six weeks later and died. His two friends were pallbearers, and they slipped a smile to each other across the coffin: "Wonder if he's found the lake yet?" When Sam had finished telling me the story, he sighed deeply and added, "I know Ed and Anne thought we did a lot for him, but they'll never realize how much we got out of it ourselves. It gave us a chance to be who we say we are." Another pause. "I'll die better now, and I'm grateful to old Ed for pointing the way."

As death marks the last boundary we cross in this earthly life, it seems important that the event be marked with connection and honor—and at times even fanfare. I remember a young mother's story about the night drive to the hospital with her dying daughter in her arms. It is one of those stories that can seem odd or unseemly to some, while to others of us it is deeply moving. The child had been terminally ill since birth, and both parents knew this was the final trip the three of them would take together. About halfway there, the father suddenly began sounding the horn and continued until they reached the doors of the emergency room. "It was not because we were in any hurry," he later said. "I simply felt I had an announcement to make: Hear ye; hear ye! Our daughter is now arriving at heaven's gates; she is joining the company of angels. Make way; make way!"

My father, who had set me on my way on that bicycle adorned with red, white, and blue streamers, would have been horrified at the very thought of making such a fuss. A reserved Presbyterian elder, he was now in the final hours of his relatively brief encounter with cancer, having unexpectedly fallen into a coma. It was the Monday after Father's Day. I had given him a red hummingbird feeder just hours before, never thinking he would not live to take it home. Family members and friends streamed in and out of his hospital room. I think they generally assumed that he was beyond knowing they were there. Most stood respectfully at the foot of the bed, offered dignified prayers, spoke softly to anyone else present, and slipped out. I was grateful that they came, but I really did not suppose he was aware of anything either. Still, for a reason I could not have put into words at the time, I knew that I did not want him to be alone, and so I sat through all the comings and goings, holding fast to a hand that did not hold back.

At some point, our Episcopal bishop entered. He gently pulled open Daddy's eyes and nodded as he released them. He firmly placed his big hands on the hairless head and literally bellowed down into him: "BENJAMIN, CAN YOU HEAR ME? BENJAMIN! I AM HERE TO BLESS YOU IN THE NAME OF THE FATHER, AND OF THE SON, AND OF THE HOLY SPIRIT! AMEN!" It seemed to me that the words went deep into Daddy's very marrow. The bishop repeated them twice. Then with great authority, he shouted the prayers for the dying, all the while massaging that bald head and calling my father by his Christian name. There was nothing tentative about this laying on of hands, and I remain confident today that Daddy heard something of the blessing, that he felt God's healing touch. The boundary must become blurry when one is so close to death. I suspect we move back and forth a bit at the time of crossing, and connection with those on either side of the line is the order of the day. Daddy breathed his last a short time later. It was a long, whispery exhalation, and it sounded perfectly normal to me. When I looked at the inert form on the bed, I knew he had gone somewhere else—passed over from life to death to life. For my own sake more than his, I am glad I was there to wish him Godspeed.

–FOUR–

Closed and Open

Boundaries afford order, protection, and identity for both people and communities. Without the consistency, safety, and meaning they provide, we would find it difficult to undertake anything new or to welcome uninvited guests into our midst. Maintaining our boundaries involves holding both sides of a tension: firmness coupled with a willingness to keep the boundary flexible and to look for alternative ways of doing things. It calls for an eye open to opportunity and the time to move ahead.

During the spring my sons were thirteen and ten, a teaching assignment in France afforded our family the opportunity of European travel. The occasional aggravations of the boys' presence (an hour in the Louvre was more than enough for them when the parks of Paris lay outside its doors!) were offset by their eagerness to dash into adventure and thus to drag their more timid mother into experiences she would not have chosen for herself. A memorable example is our visit to the Leaning Tower of Pisa.

Suffice it to say that I do not like heights. Something in me twists painfully cold when my feet are too far off the ground. The Leaning Tower is eight stories high, and nearly three hundred steps spiral up through its interior.

To David and Jonathan, these steps were an invitation to run a mad race to the top, with me following in tentative pursuit. Everything would have been fine if we could have remained inside the tower, but child-enticing openings punctuate the various floors. For me, these doorways to the encircling, columned walkways were entrances onto narrow ledges of sheer terror. Level by level, my sons would pop out and start running around the tilting circumference. I would emerge behind them and flatten my back and the palms of my hands against the marble wall, braced to shriek warnings and to pray for survival—mostly mine. You see, there was no railing or chain to prevent one from falling or leaping to the ground below. There was no tangible line to provide safety for the three of us.

I did live to acknowledge that we made it up and then down the Leaning Tower of Pisa. The boys triumphantly bought miniature replicas in the gift shop—white, plastic facsimiles that gave me a touch of vertigo even in later years. My own souvenirs were of a different kind, because our trip to Pisa led me to think about boundaries in a new way. First, I had to admit that David and Jonathan did seem to exercise a built-in sense of restraint that served them in good stead without inhibiting their zest. This observation led me to infer that God must place within each of us an inherent appreciation of limit for our protection and well-being, as well as for our gratification and delight. We are at our healthy best when we are aware of and live according to these bounds. Second, because there was no adequate boundary for me that day, I found myself unable to participate in the exhilaration of the climb to its fullest measure. For whatever reason—overriding maternal concern, previous experience, genetic predisposition—my internal mechanism either did not click in or was not up to the moment. From all of this, I concluded that awareness of boundaries is necessary for creative and full living.

–Semi-permeable Membranes–

We have seen that boundaries define who we are and who we are not, what we are to do and what we should not, what is ours and what is not, where we are to go and where we should not. We now can say more about their nature. Like a cell membrane, a boundary must be semi-permeable: admitting and containing what is necessary for sustaining and enriching life, discharging and excluding anything that does not belong within its borders. A membrane that allows anything and everything to enter and leave is a membrane that is no longer functioning. The cell—the system—is now dead or dying. A healthy boundary is firm enough to hold, but not so tight that it binds, confines, and cuts. It is flexible enough to allow movement and change within time and circumstance, but not so loose that it encourages sloppiness and aimless wandering. A boundary that is too rigid fosters stiff and brittle attitudes; it is always in danger of freezing and cracking. One that is too porous encourages attitudes of carelessness and disorder; it will rot and crumble.

A friend and I were bewailing our mutual tendency to put too much on our calendars, to agree to do too many things, even if every one of them is rewarding and good. Nancy allowed, "We are committing the sin of gluttony—in this case, the greed for experiences!" While all the food on the table may be tasty and nutritious, we are nonetheless overloading when we pile it on our plates, when we are reluctant to place limits on ourselves—when we are unwilling to accept our God-given limitations on appetite and capacity. We can find it so very difficult to say, if I am this, then I can't be that; if I am here, I can't be there; if you are there and I am here, we are not in the same place; or if I decide to do this, I cannot do that. We seem to believe that we will maintain a measure of control over our lives if we can have and do anything and everything upon which we set our longing hearts. The ironic twist is that just the opposite is true.

One way of defining addictive behavior is the inability to decide to live within certain limits or boundaries. Addicts—whether the problem lies with disorders in eating or drinking, gambling, compulsive overwork or buying—believe that they can prescribe and keep bounds for themselves. Because they can do no such thing, their lives become unmanageable. Remember, a cell membrane that freely lets everything in and out is the vehicle of the cell's destruction. It is noteworthy that the first three steps in any twelve-step program to recovery—acknowledgment of personal powerlessness to control or manage, belief in the possibility of restoration by a greater power, and the decision to turn will and life over to that power—are echoed in the vows we make at baptism:

> *Do you renounce Satan and all the spiritual forces of wickedness that rebel against God?* Do you reject those powerful influences that would have you believe you can control or manage nature and history?

> *Do you renounce the evil powers of this world which corrupt and destroy the creatures of God?* Do you reject those influences that would have you believe you can control or manage our political, economic, and social systems?

> *Do you renounce all sinful desires that draw you from the love of God?* Do you reject those influences that would have you believe you can control or manage your own life?

Do you turn to Jesus Christ and accept him as your Savior? Do you recognize him as the one who can save you by freeing you from the power of these influences?

Do you put your whole trust in his grace and love? Do you place your total confidence in his loving presence and action in your life?

Do you promise to follow and obey him as your Lord? Do you acknowledge him as the one who directs and guides your life?

As we proceed to live the lives that God intends for us, free from those binding influences that imprison us, our boundaries will be both firm and flexible. To put it another way, we can sit behind the doors of our homes, stay within the borders of our country, stand within the bounds of our rules and our beliefs, never climb the steps of the Leaning Tower of Pisa—and we can feel safe. But living unto ourselves, believing that in so doing we will be secure, protected from the powers at work out there, at the end offers only a limited view. We miss the rich color of life that is possible only as we allow ourselves to be open to all that surrounds us. We become oblivious to the connections among us and to the contributions each of us brings. We may enjoy a measure of defense within the walls of our sanctuaries, but if we do remain isolated behind them, our backs turned, we finally will suffer stagnation and the death of soul. A sturdy yet passable boundary provides windows through which those inside and those out can extend greetings to each other, apertures to let in both the bright light of day and the soft darkness of evening hours. It provides doors through which we can enter and leave when the season is right, portals that allow the fragrance of fresh breezes to pass through.

This is a good place to acknowledge that differences in personality, ethnicity, culture, and the like color the various manifestations of boundary and hospitality, and unless we take this into consideration, we run the risk of misinterpreting another's intention. For example, I am one who cringes at the thought of the family-style eating arrangements in inns to which some of my friends flock. My idea of hospitality is a small, private table in a quiet corner of the room. I do not like to be asked to stand for public acknowledgment when I am a visitor in a church. To someone else, this is a sign of warm welcome. My husband tells about a trip he took to Japan to lecture. As his host walked him to the airport gate for departure, John presented him with a small token of appreciation—an engraved silver spoon from the United States. He was stunned when the man violently shook his head from side to side and then bolted away. He returned shortly with an offering for John that he had purchased somewhere in the airport. His cultural definition of hospitality precluded accepting a gift unless he had something to give in return. Similarly, when John and I were anticipating a visit by our daughter-in-law's Cantonese parents, Wan Lan warned us ahead that they were bringing a "piece of art," and she hoped we could simply receive it and do nothing in return, otherwise we would spoil the intent of their gesture. By the way, the gift turned out to be an exquisite, long Chinese scroll, which now hangs in our stairwell, visible to all who come to the front door.

A group of brightly-clad Buddhist monks visited our church one Sunday morning. They were part of an international exchange program and came with a parishioner. I do not know whether they spoke any English, but they did seem to catch the spirit of the warm words of greeting and welcome they received before the service and during the announcement time. No one was particularly bothered by their unobtrusive snapping of a few pictures as we went along. It was an innocent, touristy thing to do, and most of us knew we had been guilty of much worse at one time or another. No harm done.

Our service leaflet contains the statement of invitation common among churches in communion with each other: "All baptized persons are welcome to receive the Holy Communion at this altar." Nice and clear if one reads and understands it. But when the ushers reached the pews in which the monks were sitting, our visitors rose in unison and proceeded to file up to the altar rail along with everyone else. They knelt and extended their hands just like everyone else. By now I was watching intently, wondering what would happen. No one administering bread and wine missed a beat. The monks were served along with everyone else. They rose, filed back to their seats, and knelt respectfully. Warm greetings again accompanied them as they moved down the center aisle and out the front door at the conclusion of the service.

For days afterward, this event prompted spirited conversation among a number of us around matters like accommodation, limit, and propriety. The bottom-line question for us was: should these Buddhist monks, who surely were not baptized Christians, have been given the sacred elements of Christ's body and blood? Did we back away from our identity and requirements when we treated them just like everyone else? That was my position at first, as the one so keen on maintaining boundaries. Then someone raised another question: "Were they worshiping? That's the key." He continued, "I think the boundary was broken on this particular day, for this particular group of people, who in their own way were respectfully worshiping with us. It was not broken for all time and for all groups on all occasions." If these same monks were to come back, we would have to say something to them, explain more about who we are and what we do. What we did this time was only in accordance with

Jesus' words about the sabbath being made for humankind and not the other way around.

But there were others who thought a polite word or
touch at the altar rail would have been better and still
would have maintained a welcoming and gracious stance.
There were those who pointed out that the accompanying parishioner—or a greeter—could have been prepared
to acquaint the monks with a service unfamiliar to them:
"I wonder how many other people haven't a clue what to
do? Maybe we need to look at our whole way of welcoming visitors and strangers." Then someone else countered, "But I could never agree with denying the body and
blood of Christ to anyone—regardless of baptism! How
could we dare do so? We don't have the right." The response: "But if we don't hold that boundary, won't membership in the body of Christ have lost its meaning? We
won't be anything but a friendly group without real standards!"

Then, a final and troubling comment came from the
man who had asked whether the monks indeed were worshiping. He reminded us that the Eucharist is the rite of a
reconciled community and that all who receive communion
are reconciled—or intend to be reconciled—with everyone
else in the room. "If we took this seriously, I suspect there
were a number of us Christians today who had less business
reaching out for the bread and the wine than those Buddhist
monks did." I immediately thought of several people with
whom I was still angry and who likely were angry with
me. There probably should be occasions when we stop after we have gone through the motions of passing the
peace. It would be more honest than thoughtlessly moving ahead.

Fortunately, we came to no agreement that day. The
questions we raised are too important for easy resolution.
Rather, we began wrestling with our "essentials"—who
we have to be, even as we open our doors to those who

want to visit for a time. And we began seeing ourselves as a community more willing to risk breaking some reasonable and responsible—though not yet agreed-upon—rules, than to risk backing down on Jesus' commandment to love and on our baptismal promise to respect the dignity of every human being. After all, in that subversive way of his, Jesus regularly manages to turn our cherished presumptions upside down. His words frequently serve to wear away the walls of our narrow compartments, freeing us to look around and see what is going on, freeing us to change our minds. The order of things in the realm of God is often disconcerting. God's order will always have an element of surprise—and of paradox. Drawing lines is never a simple matter.

–The Essentials–

A commitment to the essentials is necessary before we can properly choose how to work things out or even create and improvise within the bounds. Essentials are those basic tenets and practices—components of the boundary—of any community or any discipline that if we agree to hold to them, allow us to claim membership. They constitute the foundation on which that community or that discipline finally stands. The great commandment to love God and neighbor is an example. We could not give up our adherence to it and still say with any meaning that we are God's people, the church.

A ballet teacher I know named Susan had this to say about essentials and creativity: "I have to start with the classical moves—the rudiments—and I am very strict about it. I give my students the fundamental building blocks—the rules—without which they can never be free to become real artists—to let loose and dance. You know, like 'in whose service is perfect freedom.' I draw confidence and strength from that." Susan smiled. "Some of

the younger ones think I am just being mean. More than
once, I have heard 'old fuddy-duddy'—and worse—in
loud stage whispers. But invariably, the noisiest protest-
ers are the ones who come back later to say thanks." She
went on, "And the reverse seems to be true as well. When
I am freer in my own life—when I am allowing myself
time to be and to rest and to dream, not feeling so con-
fined and locked in—then I am a better teacher of the
rules. Freedom and discipline, discipline and freedom:
they are just opposite sides of the same coin." And we
have another of those truth-filled paradoxes.

We can take this a step further. How willing would
Susan's students be to show up and to dance hard and
well if they did not know where or when the class would
be held? Suppose they were never quite sure whether Susan would show up on time—or even show up at all? Predictable and consistent boundaries of time, place, and all
the rest serve to reduce anxiety and confusion in any
given system, whether class, family, or church. They help
establish an environment in which tough and difficult
work can go on, work for which the outcome is less than
certain. Their maintenance finally is honest and unsel-
fish. I think I learned this best from a therapist whom I
saw for a number of years. The session began on the
stroke of the hour, and he pronounced it finished forty-
five minutes later. My last-minute tries of "there's just
one more thing" were invariably met with "we'll have to
take that up next time." As a result, I came to believe that
he could be trusted, and so I grew more and more willing
to delve into the matters with which I needed to wrestle if
I was to move on with my life. Toward the end of our
work together, I suggested that maybe we could have
lunch when "all of this is over." He declined firmly but
gently: "You may want to come back." I knew he was
right.

And if our relationship with God is the most essential thing we are about as human beings, then the same principles must apply to our personal disciplines of prayer and reading scripture, as well as to our communal services of worship. What does it say about us that we cannot seem to set a regular time to be quiet, for example, and to come with intent into God's presence? Why does everything else seem to take precedence? Why do we agonize over God's apparent silence when we take so little opportunity to listen for the divine voice and to read the sacred word? Is it any wonder that visitors—and even members—find our liturgies off-putting when they are sloppily run, starting late and going on forever so that the leaders of worship can delight in the sounds of their own voices?

Those of us—and I include parents, pastors, doctors, teachers—who cannot or will not set and maintain consistent limits should not wonder why our best efforts, often carried out in a well-intentioned spirit of caring and spontaneity, so regularly seem to backfire. Many of these are "pastoral" in nature, a word that has joined my list of overworked and misunderstood ones. It seems too commonly to mean, "whatever I can do in a given situation that will help me avoid anything smacking of confrontation and possible unpleasantness." And worse, since "pastoral" has to do with church concern and care, at times we can deem it all right to do too much talking, breaking bounds of confidentiality in the process and thus losing the trust of those involved. We do well to remind ourselves constantly, it is clarity of boundary that fosters health, growth, and creativity. Sloppy and cavalier definitions are ultimately demoralizing, placing us on very shaky ground. As a colleague pointed out to me, it was only because Jesus' grasp of God's boundaries was so sure and tight that he could afford to be loose in his interpretation of specific laws. His sabbath healing was never in conflict with principles of peace and justice and compassion. Indeed, when boundary lines cross, we are to ask which ones are more in accordance with the primary ones that God draws for us. It is in that service that we find the perfect freedom to work things out.

Working things out can necessitate living with shades of gray, as we allow movement back and forth across and within the boundary, as we extend hospitality. Bob, the director of that day home for persons with HIV/AIDS, told me an unsettling story about a man who against all the rules, had begun to sleep on the front porch. Bob discovered him one morning when he came in earlier than usual to open up. The man—probably in his late thirties—was not a part of the place. In fact, nobody knew anything about him at all. Bob let things go for a while to see what would happen. Days turned into weeks, and the passing of time brought more and more clutter: shopping carts, bags, sacks of aluminum cans, rolled-up blankets, old clothes. When trash began collecting in the front yard, Bob decided it was time for a talk with his guest.

He introduced himself and learned the man's name—Otis. Bob offered to find him a place at a night shelter, but Otis adamantly refused, and so they struck a deal. Bob agreed to let him continue to sleep on the front porch, and in return, Otis agreed to keep the place clean, to be responsible for his quarters. He also agreed to bring no one with him; the deal was to be just between the two of them. The one time Bob did discover someone sleeping on the back porch, the man quickly assured him, "Otis doesn't know!" A relationship of sorts thus began. Bob and Otis found time to chat every morning before Bob opened up the home and Otis went on his circuitous way for the day. During this period, Bob's second son was born, and in relaying the good news, he learned that Otis' wife and son had killed in an accident several years before. With a catch in his voice he admitted, "I haven't been able to get myself together since. Things just aren't the same. Won't ever be for me, I guess."

Otis came into the home for the first and only time one Saturday when a program was underway. Interrupting, he asked to speak to Bob. It seems that he was an electrician by trade and realized that the air-conditioning unit was malfunctioning. They shut it down, and Otis made the necessary repairs. "He saved us a bundle," Bob recalled gratefully. The daily conversations between the two men continued after that, and Bob hoped that Otis would consider moving into transitional housing and receiving assistance with job placement. But it was not to be; one day, he moved on without a word. "I hope our paths cross again," Bob told me, "but I don't really think they will. Still I often wonder, what if I had not bent the rules and gotten to know him? What difference would it have made for me? Did it make any difference for him in the long run? And I wonder if making a difference is what it's all about, anyway. Maybe just our talking together was enough." Bob paused. "Anyway, I'm glad we did. I pray for Otis every day and hope he's okay out there. I think he prays for me. He's a good man."

In telling me this story, several times Bob used the phrase, "living in the gray." It stuck with me. He meant that the black-and-white, hard-and-fast answers are not always possible or desirable as we live with the tension between maintaining our boundaries and also making room at the altar or on the front porch—in the end, the requisite tension of all relationship. But I do not think Bob meant gray as a muddy or indistinct category, occupying a sloppy in-between range. In making the decision to allow Otis sleeping space on the porch, he acknowledged that compassion and hospitality were more essential to the operation of the day home than a strict adherence to the stated rules. A gray, middle-ground answer may be the one we can give that is most faithful to the gospel as we find ourselves pulled between standing for something and at the same time extending welcome to those who approach our doors and who draw their lines in a completely different way.

But we are wrong if we take Bob's "living in the gray" to mean that anything goes, that finally nothing matters. It is not that simple. What it does mean is that we must be rigorous in distinguishing between essentials and nonessentials in order to hold fast to the former, while working to expand our understanding of the rest. This search for essentials requires willingness to test and retest, as well as a tolerant appreciation of those who do the testing. To say it another way, the community within a particular boundary is to seek a common mind about what constitutes its core identity. But if it is to be alive and well, this community also must be one of openness to new possibilities. We climb to the height of arrogance when we claim to know all there is to know about anything. Gray can be the bright color of humility—and of hospitality.

–Plan B–

Hospitable keeping of boundaries demands flexibility—with a dash of inventiveness thrown in for good measure. While this flexibility is related to Bob's living in the gray, I do not think it is quite the same thing. Rather than striking a compromise, flexibility means coming up with an alternative route we may like even better than the original. A friend of mine has a favorite Yiddish expression she pulls out whenever things do not proceed exactly as projected: "Man plans, and God laughs." Each time she repeats these words, Marcia accompanies them with a good-natured chuckle and shrug of her shoulders. My family must go along with her philosophy to a degree, for we regularly engage in the practice of outlining plans "A," "B," and even "C" when events or consequences are important enough to warrant. Some of our plans are totally impractical; some, outright laughable: "If we miss the plane, we'll take the train; if it does not come, we can always walk—to Toledo?" Having a backup has saved the day more than once. Further, these alternative schemes do serve to remind us once again that we are finally not in control of our lives and are foolish when we begin to think and act as if we were.

To be hospitable is to expect the unexpected, to expect interruption—maybe interruption is our real work, after all—and then to proceed into the opportunity it affords with all the inventiveness and humor we can muster. There is just no telling who or what is going to show up next, and the time will never be completely convenient or good. I remember a baptismal celebration when alternative plans became the order of the day—and the occasion of truly creative hospitality—after an unwelcome guest made its literally spotty appearance.

The baby was chubby, bald, and as beautiful as they come—the rosy-cheeked pride and joy of her parents and her two older siblings. Her long, white baptismal gown had been worn by both of them, as well as by members of preceding generations. It was washed, lightly starched, ironed to perfection, and hung in a closet awaiting the big day. The calendar date had been long set to accommodate friends and relatives traveling some distance to be there—especially a godfather who would be flying in from South Africa. Her parents were hosting a luncheon in their home following the service. Flowers had been ordered and the caterer hired, and a sumptuous menu was selected. The officiating priest would complete the baptismal instruction on Saturday, after everyone had arrived. The five-day weather forecast called for a picture-perfect Atlanta spring day.

The priest's telephone rang early on Thursday morning. It was the baby's mother, with the news that Deane

had broken out with chicken pox! So what to do in the
face of this most unexpected and inconvenient caller?
There was no way they could reschedule the baptism; too
many already were en route from too far. But it could not
take place in the church on Sunday because Deane still
would be contagious, a real risk for anyone who had not
had the disease. A private baptism was not the answer;
her parents appreciated the communal nature of the rite
and did not want to undermine its significance for anyone, especially their own family.

Before long, "Plan B" began to emerge. The entire
baptismal party came to the regular eleven-o'clock service at the church: parents, sister and brother, grandparents, godparents, out-of-town relatives and friends,
in-town relatives and friends who were not members of
our congregation—everyone. Only the baptismal candidate remained at home, in the care of a longtime family
friend. We began the service as if the baptism would take
place then and there:

> There is one Body and one Spirit;
> *There is one hope in God's call to us;*
> One Lord, one Faith, one Baptism;
> *One God and Father of all.*

When we got to the place where Deane would have been
presented, the priest recounted the circumstances with
sympathy and a measure of humor. A wave of affectionate
murmurs and chuckles rippled throughout the congregation. He explained that he and others would go to Deane's
home right at the end of the service and would baptize her
on behalf of them all. He went on to say that her parents
would present her in church for the public recognition of
her baptism as soon as she recovered. Members of the
congregation then renewed their own baptismal covenant, appropriate prayers were said for the candidate and

her family and for the occasion, the peace was exchanged, and the communion followed.

Quite a group trooped over to the house afterwards: the baptismal party and invited luncheon guests, as well as the priest and several members of the altar party, including an acolyte or two. Outside on the front porch, a large and colorful sign warned anyone entering to beware of chicken pox. Candles were lit as the godparents assembled; after promises were spoken and water blessed, Deane was properly baptized and anointed—to the applause of her admiring throng. Just as the priest dipped his hand into the bowl of water, calling upon God to sanctify it, the clock passed on to the family by the baby's late great-grandmother sounded its chime, pronouncing her maternal blessing on the event. Deane seemed to feel pretty good by the time everything was said and done, and for a while, she patiently humored all who wanted to hold her and pass her around. Then when she finally had had enough, the new Christian gave up and went to sleep. The rest of us ate from the gorgeous spread on the dining room table that had been laid out in her honor.

True to their word, her parents brought her to church several weeks later and carried her down in front of the entire congregation for their welcome and more applause. I hope Deane remembers all the clapping for the rest of her life. I do not think anyone felt left out or more important, thought we cut any corners on this baptism. Hospitality meant that we held on to the essentials—the corporate nature of the sacrament—while meeting the particular needs of a family as they tried to welcome wanted and unwanted, expected and unexpected guests. Deane's mother later provided a postscript to the story. It seems the family went out of town shortly thereafter. Not quite sure what to do with the sanctified water left in the silver bowl, they put it in a safe place until their return. While away, they decided they would plant a tree to commemorate the occasion and sprinkle it with the contents of the bowl. Upon their return, however, they discovered that the water had completely evaporated into the air of the house. "I guess we'll just have to live here forever," she told me. "How could we ever sell this place now?"

Deane's story is admittedly an appealing one—a charming, low-risk chance for flexibility. The solution to the predicament is one with which few would have any problem whatsoever. Nonetheless, it reminds me of other baptisms, more complex situations that well-intentioned people tried to work out within the bounds as they understood them. For example, an interning hospital chaplain told me that she had recently baptized a stillborn baby, responding to the pleas of the devastated young parents. "The baby was a boy," Mary said. "They named him John—after his father." She knew she could be faulted for baptizing a dead body—the child was no longer there. But she figured it was a whole lot more important to God that she give the couple some measure of comfort. "Besides, I couldn't have lived with myself if I'd done anything less." Mary paused and looked down at the floor. She had not reported the incident to her supervisor yet. She said that she just was not up to dissecting it right then; to do so felt disrespectful to John and his parents. "However, maybe it's more than that for me. I know I went against the tradition and teachings of the church. Maybe I need to think about my decision before I'm faced with one like it again."

My friend Stan is an inner-city priest. As part of his community ministry, he has always walked the streets and sat around in diners, getting to know souls who likely will never enter the doors of the church but whom he nevertheless understands as members of his parish. He had had long conversations over many cups of coffee with a prostitute who worked this particular neighborhood.

She had become pregnant—the father was unknown—and had decided to keep the baby. "I guess I'm
going to have to change my profession," she said to Stan.
"It doesn't seem right now." He promised to help her look
at alternatives once the baby had come and she was ready
to get started.

A few days after the birth, Stan dropped by her spare
apartment with a bag of food and some additional baby
supplies. His friend invited him in, offered him a cup of
coffee, and nervously announced that she had a special request to make of him. "I want you to baptize
her—now—right here on my kitchen table! She and I
have got to make it right with God if we're are going to
have a fighting chance." Stan agreed and did so—in the
name of the Father, and of the Son, and of the Holy
Spirit—not yet bothering to explain that the baby was already in God's good graces. In the coming weeks, he continued to stop by and talk to the new mother about all
kinds of things, including the meaning of baptism. Before
too long, she told him that she was moving back to her
hometown to live with family. "They're Methodists, so
we'll have a place to go." There also was the prospect of a
job. "Thanks for everything," were her last words to Stan.
Later he confessed to me that he had never done anything
quite like that before. It flew in the face of much that we
hold about baptism: for starters, the baby's parents were
not active members of a Christian community, and there
were no godparents' names to record, other than Stan's.
"But," he concluded, "I've had fewer second thoughts
about this one than about many others that on the surface
were more traditional. I certainly wasn't presiding at a
social event!"

And I baptized my son David. He was sick, I was
afraid, and my theology at the time was not so much different from that of Stan's friend: we had to get right with
God. I did it all by myself in the proper Trinitarian form,

but I did not think to tell the priest when David was later presented for his "real" baptism. I did not know that his first was the real one and that it only needed to be recognized by the community at a public celebration. I have not lost much sleep over my lapse. I think God was delighted to be of special comfort and encouragement to a frightened young woman.

–Opportunity–

Shortly after Deane's encounter with chicken pox, I heard another mother talk about welcoming an uninvited guest. Alice, the parent of an autistic son, addressed a diocesan commission to invite her church, to join her family and the many others who were coping with various kinds of disabilities and seeking ways to accommodate those for whom the "normal" ways of doing things just do not work. She reminded us that all who live within a particular boundary do not have the same gifts or the same limitations. If everyone is to be received and welcomed, much less included, these boundaries must be looked at in more creative ways. Alice was making her own ardent plea for flexibility, for a willingness to develop and explore plans "B" and "C"—and sometimes even "D."

I had the idea that she did not speak in public very often. Her voice quavered a bit, and her hands were stiffly clasped in front of her on the table, knuckles white and protruding. Nevertheless, Alice's obvious nervousness only served to increase both the strength and the poignancy of her message. The attention of everyone in the room was riveted upon her. "There are so many of us out there," she said, "families who feel alone and isolated, embarrassed by what has happened to us, sure that no one wants to look at us or put up with all our disruptions." Her son Jim has to take all of his equipment everywhere he goes. It provides him with a measure of well-being, but at times it can fill up an entire pew. "And we never know when there will be a loud outburst. They usually come at the worst possible times in the service, of course—moments of silence or in the middle of the sermon. We never quite get to sit easy."

Alice stopped to catch her breath. Then as if she were seeing it for the first time herself, she suddenly said, "We have to take off all those roofs!" Some of us must have looked a bit puzzled. She forged right on with her explanation, talking very fast now. "Remember when they came to Jesus, carrying that paralyzed man on a mat? They couldn't get close to him because of the crowd; so they climbed up on the roof, made an opening through the tiles, and lowered the man down. That's what we have to do: take off the roofs—whatever they are—so we can get to him, and he can touch us, and we can have the chance to be made whole." With that image, Alice pressed us to keep our eyes open for opportunities to risk stepping beyond established and expected bounds, opportunities for wholeness.

Several years ago, I was asked to take on a challenging piece of work: to serve as the director of our diocesan pre-seminary screening program. It was an undertaking for which I had had little formal training and no direct experience and thus was one of those assignments that would force me to stretch. To complicate the situation, the person who previously had been in charge had met with a measure of resistance and criticism, and I did not know how much of this I would inherit. Even in the face of all of my doubts and anxiety, the prospect of doing "something new" still was alluring, and I agreed to give it a try. After all, what did I have to fear but public ridicule and abject humiliation? Shortly before I was to begin, a well-meaning friend took me out to lunch to confront me with my folly and warn me of the high probability of failure—as if I needed such advice. The voices in my head were doing a superb job on their own.

Despite her admonitions and my own reservations, I stayed with my resolve to have a go at it. The assignment turned out well, but that was not as important as my seeing it as an opportunity and taking it on. Humiliation was not my fate. I added my own touches to the project and received compliments of "well done," while the mistakes I made contributed to our collective wisdom as well. When the time came for me to move on, I was sincerely thanked. More important, I gained confidence and experience, and both have continued to serve me in good stead. I remain gratified that I was able to hear the stirrings of my heart over the din of the other voices—interior as well as exterior.

I later came across an ancient Muslim caveat: Four things come not back: the spoken word; the sped arrow; time past; the neglected opportunity. This old saying enticed me back into my beloved word digging. My dictionary told me that the Latin root for "opportunity" is *portus*—a harbor or haven. Remembering something I had read, I called my daughter-in-law Wan Lan, and she informed me that the Chinese words for "opportunity" and "crisis" share a common character. She went on to explain that one meaning of that character is "chance." Stirring all of this together, I inferred that every opportunity must have a measure of risk and danger, and we will be taking a measure of chance when we embrace it. But unless we do so, the harbors—the havens—of possibility and fulfillment will be closed. It will be too late for us. At the end of our conversation, Wan Lan said to me in her soft lilting way, "I think I took a great risk when I came to this country several years ago. I did not know what I would find, but it was an opportunity I could not lose."

I am afraid that I know all too well about time past and the neglected opportunity:

- I wish I had spent more time reading to my children when they were very young. People warned me, but time ran out.

- I wish I had spent more time with my grandmother before she died. I just could not imagine her not being with us forever, and time ran out.

- I am grateful that I had the opportunity to say everything to my father that I needed to say before he died. I only wish I had gotten to know him better before time ran out.

- I wish I had enjoyed my school years more, and good grades had not been so important. I could have enjoyed my education more than I did.

- Today, I hope I can slow down my life and concentrate more on my reading and my writing—before time runs out and opportunity again is lost.

Even so, taking hold of an opportunity implies a transition, the crossing of a threshold. In ancient Near Eastern religions, it was customary to leap over temple thresholds rather than step upon them. The doorsill was believed to be the habitation of spirits and thus, a dangerous place indeed. We can recognize this as wisdom; thresholds can be sites of great tension. They are those locations on the boundary where we ask the questions, where we struggle to welcome, where movement inside and out can take place if we do. They are kinetic spots of energy and restlessness, points of intersection where people and ideas can get at each other, where various views can come into conflict. An architect reminded me that while a well-constructed threshold keeps out rain and cold and blistering heat, it is also a place of danger where one can trip and fall. Both alluring and frightening, enticing and unsettling, thresholds mark those liminal times of ending and beginning when some things have to end so something else can begin. Those are the times when we find ourselves standing on a doorstep wondering whether we dare cross over or would be better off turning around and heading back the other way, to what is familiar. Neither inside nor out, thresholds are nowhere places, and even the most stalwart among us likes to be somewhere.

Still, our lives are made up of moments, milestones, and seasons of living between this and that. The moment dies just as the new one comes into being, and every time we close our eyes to go to sleep, we move toward the boundary line that marks another day. If we think about it, God's time has always seemed to involve those uncomfortable transitions between where we are and where we have not been before: the watery time before the dove returned and the rainbow appeared, the desert time between Ur and Canaan, the wilderness time between Egypt and the promised land, the time of exile between Jerusalem fallen and Jerusalem restored, the three-days time between the cross and the empty tomb, the time today in which we wait for Christ to come again. Indeed, the word "transition" comes from the Latin *transire*—to go across—to cross those boundaries of ending and beginning so new opportunity can be found:

- Like the moment we emerge from watery wombs and gasp those first breaths of air.

- Like the time the spirited water of baptism is poured over our heads and we have new names in the company of saints.

- Like the day we let go of our mother's hand and walk through those heavy school doors.

- Like the season we sense that childhood is past and responsibility will now be ours.

- Like the occasion on which we say, "I do," and two become one.

- Like the time a relationship shatters and we have to start over again.

- Like the hour we draw our final breaths and the gates of eternity swing open before us.

Jesus tells the disciples a parable about being prepared and ready for those times when we find ourselves at a threshold of opportunity. We can either cross or miss our chance altogether. Ten maidens were waiting to join a bridal procession as it passed on the way to the wedding feast at the bridegroom's house. Five of them assumed that he would arrive in daylight, and they made no provision for filling their lamps with oil. The other five knew that the bridegroom could arrive at any time, and they brought the necessary oil—just in case. The bridegroom was delayed; all ten bridesmaids became drowsy and dropped off to sleep. Then at midnight—the darkest hour, the unexpected moment—came the cry: "The bridegroom is here; the time is now; come out to meet him!" The young women leapt to their feet in anticipation of the celebration. Then five of the lamps began to flicker and go out. As the bridesmaids went off to buy oil, the procession arrived and passed on. All in its number crossed over the threshold of the bridegroom's house, and the door was closed. By and by, the foolish maidens managed to present themselves at the same threshold, but the bridegroom denied them entrance, not because they ran out of oil, but because they were not there when the moment came. Time had run out; their opportunity was forever lost.

Jesus has hard things to say about threshold crossings and lost opportunity. He is known to speak of narrow doors and narrow gates and to say that those who stand outside knocking, expecting to be let in, may find themselves disowned. He speaks of the weeping and gnashing of teeth, of the last being first and the first being last. Jesus does not say that God's grace will run out, but that time as we know it finally will. While his hard words never negate the truth of God's grace, they insist on our need to act before it is too late. We will have to cross uncertain thresholds and *strive* to enter through the door that is narrow indeed. From Jesus' word for strive comes the English word "agony." The way of the disciple is the way of his cross—the way of suffering love, the way of power that is vulnerability.

We Christians claim our identity as threshold people every time we make that assertion about Christ's dying and rising and coming back again. We affirm that we can live with the uncertainties of this day and every day because we know the final outcome. But threshold living is not the same as marking time, forever hovering. It is more like balancing on the end of a diving board. We hesitate; then at the fitting moment, we make our resolve, take a deep breath, and spring up and off, sailing into the sky. Cold feet need not constrain us to crawl back down the ladder, paralyzed by hopelessness and fear. We need not be pushed or prodded or bribed; we can believe in new possibilities. Our God reigns from the empty arms of the cross. Our God has gone before and has shown us the way. Our God will cross with us. Our God is waiting on the other side.

Moving and Changing

> *If a boundary defines, then moving or removing that boundary means redefinition. Something new is being identified and named. The work of changing a boundary—or moving ourselves across a threshold—demands attention and a willingness to listen to the voices around us.*

I came upon the intricate web of a large spider the other day. It stretched from the low branch of a dogwood tree, right across the path where I was walking, to the spires of my neighbor's rosemary bush. Fortunately, I saw it in the nick of time and was able to avoid demolishing the creature's gossamer domain in my haste to get to my own home. It would have been a shame to destroy—albeit unintentionally—something so beautiful that had taken so much time and effort. Besides, I did not have the right: the lines of that web marked the spider's earlier claim to the space. I carefully ducked under it and continued on my way. This time, I was spared the shock of gauzy remains suddenly plastered to my hair and face, as well as the accompanying twinge of guilt as I pictured the poor spider weaving its home all over again.

A similar thing can happen when I carelessly barge into another person's territory. One day I had been trying to get one of the priests in our diocese—Dan—on the telephone all morning, and my frustration was mounting. A conversation with him was necessary before I could make another call, which would remove a pesky piece of business from my desk. Suddenly, I heard Dan's voice in the hall; he was talking to the man who occupies the office next door. I was elated. I jumped up and hurried out. "Am I interrupting you?" I stupidly asked. Of course I was! The two men offered a polite, "No, not at all," and I plunged ahead with my question. Dan answered it, and I scurried back to my room to make the waiting call. My hall neighbor later expressed his displeasure. I offered an apology and my lame explanation, and we cleared the air between us. "Don't let me get away with that again," I begged him. Sometimes I am just blind to the obvious. The spider web was a near miss. With this interruption, I managed to plunge on through another line without any right to do so.

These are illustrations of boundaries that are moved—or nearly moved—inadvertently or by accident. It can happen when we are not paying adequate attention to our surroundings, when we are preoccupied with our own concerns and not aware of others in our midst. Apologizing and resolving to look around and to listen more respectfully may be the only recourse open to us in the aftermath of our bull-in-a-china-shop intrusions. More serious is the tragic destruction of lines in times of crisis, by flood and fire, illness and death—events that initially are out of our hands. In their wake, we must pick up the pieces and move on, calling on every resource we have at our disposal, human and divine. Last of all are the boundaries that we deliberately decide to change, the thresholds we consciously decide to cross. We make such decisions when the old ways are not working for us anymore, when the old walls are too confining—or not confining enough.

—Making Changes—

My father loved to tell a story on himself about moving a boundary that was no longer working for him. Daddy grew up in a very small town in southwest Georgia. The eldest of five children, he was the one on whom his parents learned their child rearing. My grandmother Bessie—a cautious woman by nature and a total non-swimmer in fact—had handed down her sensible law in no uncertain terms: Daddy could not go swimming until he knew how to swim. Now just outside town, there was a deep pool formed by the icy waters of some natural springs. This was the local children's swimming hole. During one particularly blistering summer, Daddy's longing to join them in their cold, shrieking fun exceeded his will to mind his mother's rule. The catch: he could think of no way he could learn to swim without just taking himself to those beckoning waters and plunging in. He did, and he swam. In doing so, he had stretched and extended his personal boundary, added another page to his history. "Swimmer" had become one of the words that gave him identity; he was included in the line encircling the other children.

But Daddy had yet to reckon with his mother, and to his credit, he did so in the most direct manner possible. When he arrived home that momentous afternoon, hair still damp, he simply announced, "Mother, I can go to Nancy Springs; I have learned how to swim!" While I do not know what the consequences were, I am sure he suffered something at the hands of my grandmother. I am also sure that he never regretted his line-changing

action. Many years later, Grandmother Bessie did confess that she was relieved to have one less thing to worry
about, that she was glad to have her son a part of the
swimming community.

Unlike Daddy, my friend Edith did not give much
thought to the boundary with which she so merrily tam-
pered: the number of guests they could realistically include in her daughter Liz's wedding reception in Seattle.
Lists flew back and forth across the country, growing
longer and longer with every transcontinental passage.
The rule had become "no one suggested by either of the
two families could be left out," and so it would be fair to
say that this boundary had swelled out of control. Edith
at last called a halt: "If this keeps up we will not be able to
afford to do anything except serve ice water and saltines.
There will be no decent party for anyone!" She established a new rule, giving both families a specific number
of guests they could include on their list. Substitutions
were allowed, as long as the total number stayed the
same. And she stuck to her guns. Teasing her I moaned,
"I guess this means I'm not invited." "Right!" she said,
"but at least you won't have to fork over a present." Edith
had come right up against our caveat about boundary and
hospitality: we must have something to which we can invite others before we can extend meaningful and gracious
invitations. If things had kept on the way they were heading, Liz's wedding reception would only have been a mob
scene.

In the public arena, prohibitions on sexual harassment
is one example of our coming to terms with old ways that
are not serving us well—of our changing the rules. We
have decided that employees' endurance of ridicule and
distasteful humor or the sexual advances of higher-ups
for fear of losing jobs or promotions is not to be tolerated.
We are coming to understand such cases as mistreatment
involving the abuse of power. In preventing them, we are

maintaining that each and every one of us—regardless of our place in the system—is to have the final say about where her or his personal boundary of comfort and propriety lies. Someone else is not to draw that line. Similarly, clergy are setting limits on the number of times they will see parishioners for counseling and recognizing that it can be inappropriate for them to date members of their congregations because of the potential for abuse of power. And as we work together to redraw the old lines in more suitable places, we will experience inevitable awkwardness: Is it all right to tell that story? Is it within bounds to give him a hug? We also will worry about losing the precious spontaneity inherent in our just being together.

While we can change the rules and thus move a boundary, we should always do so deliberately and with purpose. Any decision to include or exclude either creates a different system altogether or modifies the existing one. Indeed, revolution itself might be defined as the setting of a new boundary. Responsible shifting of boundaries requires our asking a number of questions: Where is the boundary? Who or what determined it in the first place? Is this line of God, or was it set by powers acting contrary to God's will? Does there need to be a line drawn here, where there was none before? How do we know? The answers we make to these questions can help us discern when and where boundaries need to be maintained, shifted, or abolished altogether, especially concerning those areas of human life in which there is considerable disagreement. For example, we can apply the similar questions to the issue of abortion: What is the line that determines the existence of a human being? Who or what draws this line—is this line of God? About what does a woman have the right to decide? What about the rights of the fetus? We need to ask like questions about the nature and placement of lines as we consider whether or not the church should bless the relationships of homosexual men and women. Answers do not come easily. They will emerge only after intense work in personal and communal discernment—prayer, wrestling with God's word in scripture, honest exchange.

The promises of our baptismal covenant provide a plumb line against which to consider the rightness of a particular boundary:

Does this boundary enable us to continue in the apostles' teaching and fellowship, in the breaking of bread, and in the prayers? Does it help us live with each other in community—to learn and eat and pray together? Does it offer us opportunity to talk together and to grapple with our differences? Or does it serve to keep us separate and apart?

Does this boundary aid us in resisting evil and, whenever we fall into sin, in repenting and returning to the Lord? Does it encourage us to look at ourselves honestly and to make our confessions and ask for forgiveness? Does it support our being open to doing things differently? Or does it abet our keeping on those blinders of pride?

Does the very existence of this boundary attest to the Good News of God in Christ? Does it summon us to reflect the image of God in everything that we say and do? Does it assist us in proclaiming God's message of love and freedom and hope to all that we meet? Or does it prompt us to affirm the status quo—the doing of business as usual?

Does this boundary enable us to seek and serve Christ in all persons, loving our neighbor as ourselves? Does it help us see the image of God in all others and to love them as God does? Does it enable us to do everything that we can for their good—even when it works against our own? Or does it encourage us to see only their faults and blemishes and thereupon, to judge them harshly?

Does this boundary witness to justice and peace among all people, and help us to respect the dignity of every human being? Does it affirm that in God's eyes, no station is higher than any other, that all are due equal share in God's abundance? Does it summon us to welcome strangers and enemies into our midst? Or does it uphold the old hierarchies and the old ways of dividing things up?

There are lines we must change or must establish for the very first time if we are to get on with our lives and maintain our integrity as God's people—no question about it. And while we may hope that the breaking of certain rules—the challenging of certain boundaries—may eventually lead to their removal, we must be willing to take the consequences of our actions. We must be willing to be held accountable even when we passionately believe that we are on the side of the angels. Such was a critical part of the legacy left to us by Martin Luther King, Jr. Dr. King saw the laws enforcing racial segregation as wrong. He broke those laws, and he went to jail. When he came out, he broke them all over again—fully aware that to jail he would return. To follow his example is courageous work of heart and mind, work we need to continue as the lines he sought to erase still imprison us.

My Eastern European neighborhood companions and I are conspirators in a tiny revolution of our own. Little by little, I notice them starting to reemerge on their old walking trail, usually entering through a rear entrance to the office park. They bring their newspapers in plastic bags and sit reading on benches and swings in the back woods, chatting together amiably. They wave at me as I pass by, and one man even called out, "Looking good!"

The encouragement felt great. I stopped and discovered
that his name is Michael. "Mine is Caroline," I responded,
and we solemnly shook hands in a gesture of solidarity.
The language barrier may not be as constraining as I had
assumed. My jogging buddy has also starting cutting
through a back loop. He flashes his gold-toothed smile
and gives me the familiar thumbs-up greeting as we pass.
So far, we have not been caught.

–Something New–

If a boundary defines something to which we can point
and give a name, then altering that boundary means
something new is now identified—or at least emphasized
for the time being. For a number of years, I worked with a
variety of women's groups around the church. One event
I will always vividly recall took place in an Episcopal diocese in the middle of the United States. I had just finished
introducing the idea of three legitimate areas for our ministries: our personal lives, the intimate circle of family and
close friends; the world, defined as the larger community
in which we live and work; and the institutional church.
While all three deserve attention, I had explained, our
personal lives and the world around us should be the primary focus of the laity, not the institutional church. I also
cautioned that we realistically can direct attention to
only one or perhaps two of these areas at any given time,
depending upon circumstances, personal need, and the
stages of life in which we find ourselves. For example, a
young mother's main ministry is in her home, and she
should not feel guilty for saying no to other requests
made of her.

As I spoke, I became aware of a woman sitting in front
of me, weeping. Her lined face could have been described
as "full of character," giving testimony to a less than easy
life. Something about the way she held her head and the

set of her mouth suggested to me that she did not express her feelings freely or often, but at this moment, softening tears were streaming down her cheeks. I stopped speaking; actually, I did not know what to say. One hundred women became silent and waited with me. She finally spoke. "I'm already doing it. You are telling me that I'm already doing it." My eyes filled with tears too. Very softly I responded, "Yes, that is what I'm saying." The woman went on, oblivious to her surroundings. "I'm already serving Jesus! I thought you were going to tell me something else I had to do. But I can't. I've got too much already." With those few words, she summarized the day's message, and I could feel a wave of relief sweep over the room as others heard it too and received permission to tighten their self-imposed boundaries of time and energy. Somone later told me that the woman who spoke had once aspired to be an artist but long ago had been forced to give up that dream. At the present, she supplemented her income by decorating—painting—cakes. What is next for her now? I wondered.

As a boundary is tightened or moved inward, the original system becomes smaller and must be looked at differently. We begin considering a tree rather than the entire forest. For example, when a boundary is drawn more closely around a local church and no longer includes the judicatory or the wider community, members of the congregation are able to concentrate on ministries and concerns they were in danger of neglecting before. One church known for its innovative work in outreach in one of our large cities, wondering why young families were not flocking to its doors, pulled in for a time and paid overdue attention to their programs of education for children and newcomers. The result should not have been a surprise to anyone: new families began to swell the rolls. The danger lies, of course, in keeping that inward focus too long, to the detriment of their work in the city.

The tension they must struggle to maintain balances the two—outreach and self-care. Otherwise, they could succumb to the error of not seeing themselves as part of that wider community in which they do reside. This is a common pitfall for larger churches with plentiful resources: they perceive themselves as autonomous, needing little or no contact with other congregations, and thus become isolated.

Similarly, when the family or the individual concentrates solely on particulars—their own health and well-being—larger concerns can be neglected. They can lose sight of their connections to others as they come to see themselves as the center of everything. This self-centeredness could have been a danger for the weary woman in our previous story as she expanded her understanding of ministry and started letting up on her expectations of herself, no longer needing to respond to every request for her time and energy. Given her history, however, I am not too worried. My sabbatical provided me an occasion to focus on the soundness of my spiritual, physical, and mental health. Nonetheless, it could not have gone on forever. I would have lost sight of the larger spheres where I live and do my work—and where I receive so much that nourishes me.

As a boundary is expanded, new concerns and emphases arise. A smaller system is now part of a larger one, and we begin looking around at the forest where our tree grows. In other words, we consider the neighborhood where we reside or we look at the larger diocese or judicatory of which our church is a member or we take into account the world to which our country belongs. As the boundary widens, the tree, the family, the congregation, or the nation no longer exists in its own right alone. Each now must see a wider context and be aware of its interactions with its surroundings, of its dependency on the other parts of the system, if all are to survive and prosper.

Think of the only child who goes off to school for the first time, suddenly finding herself in the company of scores of other children with whom she must reckon. Or the star student from a rural high school who enters a large university and finds himself a small frog in its mammoth pond. Whether or not we consciously choose all the changes and redefinitions of boundary that occur around us, it is up to us to decide how we will react to and deal with them.

This past fall, I led a weekend event on the subject of boundaries for a group of our diocesan administrators. One of them—Cynthia—reminded us about the often-overlooked repercussions of a congregation's growth in size, another kind of boundary that is moving and changing. She has experienced these shifts firsthand in the church for which she works, and she began by describing the initial, wonderful, at-home feeling to it all when the congregation is new or small. At this stage, people are contributing all sorts of things—furniture, supplies, books—and they often retain some level of claim to what they bring in. There is a spirit of shared ownership, so that borrowing anything from office paper to a table is perfectly all right: "This really belongs to all of us." And maybe it does—for a while anyway. But as the church becomes larger and more complex, this "making ourselves at home" attitude does not work as well. Things are not always where they should be for staff and other members, and frustration begins to take its toll. Cynthia both reassured and warned us that while clearer expectations can be established without too many misunderstandings, it does take some work—some redefinition of what the church has become.

At certain times, connections among the parts of a system are more clearly realized than at others, and the boundary swings out more widely to encompass a larger whole. Often a crisis prompts this change. When the rector of a small, outlying church was diagnosed with lymphoma, the entire diocese was caught up in his plight and that of his family and congregation. Brian's treatment required that he be out for a long period of time, and a large, inner-city parish that was not particularly known for its participation in diocesan affairs was moved to offer what help they could. Every month, the church dispatched another of their priests to conduct weekly services and attend to pastoral needs. When Brian finally died, the clergy from his sister congregation took part in the funeral, and many of her parishioners sat in the overflow chairs on the grounds.

I know that members of Brian's parish still are grateful for the assistance they received, but I believe the real benefit was and can be to the ones who reached out to them. They now have opportunity to redefine themselves as members of a wider system—the household of Christ's body. Such redefinition could mean their becoming more involved in the larger church, offering their considerable resources to other, smaller congregations. It would also mean their having to take a risk: this more expansive web of relationships must then be taken into account as they make decisions about how they spend their time, energy, and money. The other option, of course, would be to resume their previous understanding of themselves as an island in the diocese—pulling that boundary back in around themselves again, not being involved to any great extent in the doings of the larger body. I wonder which direction they will choose.

–*Strange Voices*–

Sometimes, we are not so much altering or shifting a boundary as we are moving ourselves inside or outside its domain—crossing a threshold if you will. Once again, we are to proceed mindfully and with purpose. As we step over that boundary, we will find ourselves in a new place, with fresh surroundings to be explored and named. The cue that it is time to move can come from unfamiliar or unexpected sources, from strangers and voices out of the blue.

My son David called on the phone a while back to recount a late-night encounter in the parking lot of a fast-food establishment somewhere in Tennessee. He spoke very fast—even for him—and the breathless quality of his words told me that he was calling to report something of consequence. David had graduated from college several years earlier with a major in English but had remained unclear about his future direction. At the time, he was employed in an outdoors store in Chapel Hill, work he enjoyed thoroughly but knew was dead-end. This particular Sunday night, he was headed back to North Carolina after a soul-feeding weekend of bluegrass music. He had pulled off the road for a cup of black coffee, and as he walked back toward his truck, a toothless old man appeared out of nowhere and struck up a conversation. He asked David who he was and what he was up to. David later could not remember much about the first part of their exchange; knowing him, I suspect his mind was on the weekend's festival. After he responded, a long silence ensued before the old man said, "You're going to be a teacher, son, and it's high time you got started!" Then he vanished as quickly as he had appeared. The usually take-things-in-stride David described himself as shaken. "It was so weird, Mom. He came out of nowhere and talked about my future; he told me what I'm supposed to do. I keep hearing his voice running around in my head. How does he know—unless he's a prophet?" David still includes this encounter in his realm of wonder.

Now a prophet is not so much a teller of fortunes, a reader of palms or tarot cards. Prophets are those who speak on behalf of someone or something else, telling the truth as they perceive it. In the Bible, prophets are those who speak for God. When prophets of God predict events to come, they are really describing God's intentions for the present and the future. I do not know whether David actually thought his unexpected visitor might be one, but I remain convinced that somehow the old man saw or heard something of David's essence—the truth about him. David must have thought so too. Shortly after that night, he enrolled in a master's program to pursue the necessary requirements for teaching. At the time of our conversation, I lacked a concrete answer for David's question—"How did he know?"—and I continue to be without one today. However, my subsequent reflections have only served to reinforce a strong conviction: we must attend to all sorts of voices if we hope to move into the future God intends for us and for our communities. Or to say it a little differently, you hear what you listen for.

I met a woman at a recent conference who admitted to hearing voices. Of grandmotherly age, she seemed to be a conventional churchgoer, one who cares about things like religious education and parish life. She did not strike me as an oddball of any sort, yet here she was, standing right up in public and talking about her encounter with a voice. As part of the conference, we were all describing those moments when everything changed for us, and she eagerly offered her story. She began by explaining that she had suffered from crippling shyness for as long as she could remember; it rendered her unable to speak a word in front of even a small group of people. She knew that her reticence cut her off from a lot of opportunities, but she had come to accept the fact that she was just made that way.

Then one day—in the bright light of the middle of the day—while she was out doing a series of errands and alone in her car, she was startled to hear a distinct voice from the back seat telling her, "Speak out!" She turned around, and of course, there was no one there. The seat was empty; she was still quite alone. Pulling herself together, she drove on a little farther and heard it again. The message was the same. Fortunately, the woman never tried to make logical sense of it all; she probably could not have done so. But when she recounted her experience to me, she used the word "healed," and she had no doubt that the voice she heard had come from God. It told her that she could move out of the silence of shyness that had bound her all those years. She made an appointment with her parish priest as soon as she arrived home and requested training to be a reader in their services of worship. She later went on to teach some classes. "Who knows what's next?" she laughed. "Maybe I'll run for mayor!" More seriously, "What I do know is that I would not be here talking to you today if I had not listened to that voice."

I think most of us would be reluctant to stand up in an assembly of friends or strangers and admit that we hear voices—much less that we do what they tell us to do! In this day and time, such behavior might get us committed. But we do well to remember that our biblical forebears had their dreams and visions, their burning bushes and angelic visitations, and that saints and mystics have always received information in extraordinary ways. We can try to pass these revelations off as constructs of ancient and quaint storytellers, as figments of overactive imaginations or even deranged minds. However, I think we are better served by acknowledging that there are realms of awareness and possibility that far transcend anything we can know and talk about.

I have never experienced anything as dramatic as the appearance of David's prophet or a voice coming from a back seat companion. Yet for as long as I can remember, I have been aware of contacts and connections that go beyond those immediately available to my five senses or even to my intuition. I call them stirrings and biddings—or urgings, promptings, inclinations, and the like—and late August is the season when I am often most aware of them. It is that strange and unsettling time when my awareness of lost opportunity and things ending pushes right up against my expectation of fresh starts and new beginnings. The heavy air hums with the steady end-of-the-summer cadence of cicadas emerging from shed skin. Their music does not let up; it is the rhythm of late August. And while they beat out a meter of expectation and new life, their songs also announce impending death. Even as they come forth, the cicadas do not have long to live. They will sing and breed, and then they will die.

Late August is not a simple season. It is neither summer nor fall, and I hang suspended somewhere in between. The play and dreams and innocence of spring and summer are over and gone. Too soon. It is too late to make up for lost hours, lost loves, lost hopes—never to come again exactly as they were. Yet just as late August marks ending, it also offers the allure of something just around the corner, tuned to an unbearably sweet pitch. Just as I become acutely aware of my dying green spring, I am thrust onward by the stirrings around and within me. After all, late August is back-to-school time, and the ending and beginning of our church year looms as well. The child within me prepares for the start of another cycle of challenge and promise as she has always done over my span of years. She gathers her notebooks and pencils into her book bag. She puts on her new shoes, soon to be scuffed beyond recognition in real-life skirmishes. She picks up her fresh lunch box, splendidly adorned with her favorite character of the day—a protective talisman. And she sets off—again. Late August: cusp of ending and beginning—time between what is and what will be—liminal or threshold time. It is no wonder I become so aware of the haunting rhythm of the living but dying cicadas and of my own stirrings and biddings.

These stirrings and biddings—these nudging voices—that catch our attention and make us pause and wonder, beckon us across thresholds and through narrow doors. I do not know what they are like for you. For me, they take a variety of forms—like words and phrases that come from nowhere and then begin to form a pattern in my mind: "Wait...be still...trust...be patient...move!" Of strange and unsung notes from beyond my usual world of sound that leave me disquieted and unsettled. Of songs from bygone days that relentlessly play in my head: "Don't fence me in"; "Rock of ages, cleft for me"; "When you wish upon a star." Makes no difference who you are. They come when I least expect them—and sometimes when I least want them. They come when I am too content with what is and have ceased to ask what can be. Or come when I do not want anything new to re-place the old and the comfortable, when I do not want to go somewhere else. They may come when pieces do not seem to fit together any longer, when trickles of restless-ness begin to erode my walls of certainty, when I begin to look over my shoulder for someone or something to ap-pear. And they frequently come at night, when the boundary between heaven and earth grows blurry.

Stirrings and biddings may lead to daily struggles to read and write and pray, urgings to learn or teach some-thing new, promptings to write that letter or make that phone call, impulses to make an unlikely friend or to go somewhere I have never been. Over the years, they have also involved making hard decisions: having a child, tak-ing a job, leaving a job, leaving a marriage, moving, mar-rying for a second time. But the most potent yearnings these days seem to involve allowing myself just to be still and quiet and to listen. To set myself in silence, so I can hear the rustlings and whispers around me. I have all

kinds of ways I resist crossing the thresholds my stirrings and biddings reveal: *Who, me? Why me? I'm not
trained. It's not my thing. I'm too young. I'm too old. Girls
can't. Women shouldn't. Lay people don't. I'm tired. I'm
scared. I'm doing my share already. I don't have enough time.
Well, maybe next year.* Yet I am coming to know that unless
I respond to their nudgings and consider crossing over
into whatever lies ahead, I risk never becoming who God
intends me to be, never offering what I can on this day's
doorstep. When I am afraid that I am ill equipped to handle whatever lies on the other side of that door, I remember that God has frequently placed improbable people in
unlikely situations. I am in good company.

So if I am honest and say what I really believe, I will
call at least some of these stirrings and biddings divine
interruptions into my life. I will acknowledge them as the
messages of divine voices. But how can we know whether
the words we hear are from God or whether they are
products of our flawed longings—or worse? Are they
whispers from heaven or the murmurings of hell? A wise
man offered me the following counsel as I struggled with
the threshold-crossing decision of whether to follow my
inclination and leave a job before knowing what would
come my way next. He said, "When the promise is clear
and the cost is vague, watch out; the evil one may be woo-
ing you. But when the cost is clear and the promise is
vague—yet there is something that is alluring, something that draws you forward—watch out. You may be
hearing the voice of God." *Clear cost—vague promise—voice of God.*

When we look back over the story of the people of
God, many of its chapters seem to start out with a vague
promise and a clear sense of cost. Abram and Sarai leave
family and homeland to set off on that journey across the
desert to God knows where. The disciples drop everything and follow Jesus into God knows what. The blinded

Saul, hit by that divine two-by-four on the road to Damascus, stumbles into the house on the street called Straight and waits for God knows whom. And even though we have been granted a glimpse of our story's glorious conclusion, even though we know that God's final promises are splendid indeed, we are not exempt from the sweaty palms and thumping hearts of those who have gone before. We want to know how all the in-between places will turn out, to be sure that the cost will not be too dear. We want to be able to change our minds before it is too late to turn back. We want to say how it will be at the end. But such desires are born of our need to know and too often to control the outcome. God does not promise that we can determine results and consequences; God only promises that we will not be alone. Even so, it is difficult for us simply to believe that God is interested in us, a presence in all that we are and everything that we do.

–Familiar Prophets–

Sometimes, those voices urging us to move a boundary or cross a threshold are the ordinary ones right in our midst—ones we tend to dismiss because they are familiar or expected. These voices include but are not limited to those of our designated leaders. We might say that leadership's place is at or near the system's boundary, looking at what is going on both inside and out. I have always appreciated leaders who were brave enough to draw lines, welcome reactions to them, and later had the courage to move or erase their lines when time proved them wrong. When leaders are doing their job of keeping watch over the whole, they will notice matters we need to address, ideas and people we need to consider and even take in. They will pay attention to who is leaving and who is staying, what is being talked about and what is being shoved under the carpet. They will ask questions about decisions and direction—prophetic questions about our identity and whether or not we are being true to it. Remember, prophets are those who proclaim what God's plan has been all along and beckon us to join in.

But prophecy is not limited to leadership. Fortunately so, for sometimes leaders are too bound up in the success or survival of the system as it is—family, church, school, city, nation—to risk moving things around. Crucial questions are also asked from corridors or corners or even from beyond the threshold—from meal tables, classrooms, hospital beds, and community shelters: Why do we? Why don't we? Have you ever thought about it? Why not? Things could be different, you know. They are asked by children at play and grandparents at prayer, by newcomers and those who come around infrequently—by a redheaded stranger passing through Atlanta, looking for a place to take a shower and wash her clothes. Those on the other side of the boundary always see from a perspective we cannot; they know what is hidden from our eyes until we let them show us. They meet us on our sidewalks and at our doors. They quite literally stand on our thresholds—the ancients' habitation of spirits. They call us to deal with that tension between boundary and hospitality, to answer questions about identity and membership, cost and promise. Otherwise, we will not learn enough about ourselves—and they will not know whether to cross over or step back to be better served somewhere else. And we do well to remember that when the door is other than our own, we become the threshold voices asking for a hearing. Things always look different from the other side.

Further, we should not count the number of voices before giving them credence. Even one—a minority report—is enough to merit attention. After all, who is wise enough to pinpoint the source of every word? So I would include among the crucial voices those who speak up and make certain everyone gets a chance to be heard—teachers and guides, translators and interpreters, those who take minutes and draft reports, those who write down the stories and draw the pictures of our times. I would include those in the community who help us sort through our own stirrings and biddings—parents and pathfinders who stay with us and give us frank and candid support as we wrestle with bearing and course. And sometimes, the voice will be our own. I recently heard about a woman who found herself on her feet, speaking out in the middle of a sermon, much to her own surprise and the dismay of the preacher. He told me the story.

The church was a medium-sized one in a rather conservative, middle-sized city. Although the congregation might have characterized itself as leaning toward liberal, it had its fair share of members who took various sides of the issues of the day. The time was the early seventies, and turmoil abounded wherever one chose to look. It ran the gamut from the war in Vietnam and civil rights to liturgical renewal and women's ordination—take your pick. On the home front, this church's very active outreach committee had finally gone one step too far for some, placing a controversial advertisement in the local newspaper that said, "Come as you are!" An accompanying illustration featured a black sheep somewhat resembling a Black Angus bull. A prominent woman in the parish sent a letter to all its members, taking on the committee and declaring its work "overreach." She likely would have used the word "traditionalist" to describe herself: one who cares about what has gone before and wants to make sure it is preserved for the generations to come.

Suffice it to say that the situation did not make it easy for the rector to assume the pulpit on the following Sunday. Frank was preaching on one of the passages in which Jesus accuses the Pharisees of abandoning the commandments of God in their zealous adherence to the letter of the law. His less than subtle message was that good church people today might also make the error of caring too much about their own cherished laws. Suddenly in mid-sermon, the unthinkable happened. The woman raised her hand for recognition, rose from her seat, and in a polite but authoritative voice challenged him: "And tell me, have we been so wrong all these years?" Time stopped still—and so did the preacher. Telling the story on himself Frank recalled, "All hell broke loose while I just stood up there and shook. It was one of those times when I was awfully glad we wear vestments and no one could see my knees!"

Believe it or not, the members of the congregation next began to talk back and forth among themselves right then and there. There were some raised voices and tears and pointing of fingers, and a crazy quilt of ideas and feelings and opinions was let loose right on the spot. After a time, Frank regained a measure of composure and asked, "The Eucharist is supposed to be the sacrament of unity. So what do we do: Pack up and go home—at least for now—or continue with the service?" The congregation fumbled around for a while and then took their seats. Before long, they stood as one for the Nicene Creed, together reaffirming their faith, and for the prayers of the people, and they dropped to their knees for the confession of sin. They passed the peace and continued with holy communion. The eventual outcome of the day—even with the predictable false starts—was that people with differing views began really paying attention to each other. The parish became increasingly deliberate in its intention to welcome all comers, while at the same time trying to determine and hang on to those things it considered essential to its identity.

Only in retrospect did our traditionalist woman come to realize that her interruption had been most untraditional, and she continued on in the same vein. Ever remaining that invaluable thorn in her parish's side, she became the first woman elected junior warden in any of the city's Episcopal churches. She then became the first woman senior warden at the same time the diocese ordained its first woman priest in her very church. She hosted a reception for the new priest in her home. Not bad for a card-carrying traditionalist prophet in a leaning-toward-liberal church. Even thinking about filling her shoes is a tall order indeed.

-Transition Time-

A transition involves moving boundaries or crossing thresholds. It is the passage from what has been to what will be, from the past to the future, and pausing regularly to balance on today's threshold is the key to facing those unknowns of tomorrow. We can hope to move ahead with wisdom and courage only as we risk surrendering to the backward and forward pulls of the threshold spirits right under our feet. Transitional time and space then become necessity, never luxury, if we are to welcome the enemy and the stranger—to weigh the fear and the hope, the cost and the promise. God is always doing something. Our job is to cooperate with the divine initiative, to reach out, unlock, and open doors still shut to God, doors we might never choose on our own. Even though it is God who gives us the inclination to be about this work, it nevertheless takes intention and practice—rather like my father's learning to swim. We have to find or shape an environment in which we can listen to the voices and sort things out.

When my friend Jeffrey, an Episcopal priest, resigned his job as director of a social service agency, the tempo of his life took on a different beat. He used the transitional break well, rediscovering a sense of personal rhythm lost during those last months of employment. He played with his two small sons, prepared family meals, and painted his house. As Jeffrey began to think ahead about crossing into the next chapter of his work, he considered how he could hold on to what he had learned during the pause he had so enjoyed. He wondered how he could avoid slipping back into the old patterns that had not served him well. Another wise man gave him three suggestions. "First," he said, "figure out what went wrong before, what you would choose not to repeat. Second, provide yourself with a memory of what went well for you in the interim and go back again and again to relive it. Third, use your recollections to structure differently the new place you will be entering."

Jeffrey took the man's advice seriously and came to see that there had been virtually no boundaries in his former job. Who would be making decisions was never certain; written budgets were fragmentary at best; expectations regarding deadlines were unrealistic; standards for working through conflict were nonexistent. Further, Jeffrey had not drawn his own lines between work and personal life. He invited phone calls at all hours, too frequently grabbed meals on the run, and became more and more unavailable to his family. Any time for study and prayer had long since evaporated. In contrast, his months off had provided him with opportunity to reestablish his priorities and to feel more in charge of the hours of his day. In seeking a new position, he vowed both to be firm about what he would and would not do and to be active in helping whatever system he joined draw those lines for itself. While some may find it ironic, Jeffrey's decision was to go back into parish ministry, where he reports being happy as a clam.

I thought about Jeffrey's experience as my sabbatical leave drew to a close and it was time to return to my routine. While on the surface it would be the same work in the same place, my priorities had shifted, and I did not want to lose my determination to make ample room for writing, exercise, and prayer. What would be the consequences of my continuing resolve? What would I have to change? What resistance might I encounter? The possibility for transformation comes as we are willing to hesitate at the door before us—especially if it is one we would like to avoid. It comes as we are willing to stand squarely on the questions that door raises and to listen. This kind of stance is not passive. It requires our turning down—or better, turning off—the distractions that get in the way of our hearing and seeing. Being tuned in to the present is demanding work.

Watery images often come to my mind when I reflect on transitions. I think this has to do with water being the baptismal symbol of dying and rebirth, of passing from death to life. On some occasions, I have the terrifying sense of making my way across a high suspension bridge—a slender strand flung out between two firm lines of land. All that is real for the moment is the place beneath my feet, and I pray it will hold until I can reach the other side. Still, I often deliberately make my way to the water—to give myself over to its restorative powers and to gaze again at the steadying line of the horizon. One significant transitional time began when I was riding in the prow of a boat—and in the rain to boot.

Working as a consultant at a convention in New Orleans, I found myself at loose ends one afternoon when the delegates were occupied in a variety of routine legislative sessions. Unfortunately, the day was gray and drizzly, and ambling through the city streets was not very appealing. Then I thought of a tourist attraction that I had not yet struck from my list: an excursion ride on a paddlewheel steamboat. I headed off for the dock. There was no line when I bought my ticket; I boarded and found myself virtually alone. I climbed the steep stairs, made my way to the bow, and claimed the very front seat. I took off my shoes, tucked my long skirt under me, and hung my legs over the railing. Then we—apparently just the captain and I—left the bank behind and rode out into the Mississippi River rain. I experienced a wonderful feeling of being set free—let loose. I imagined myself to be a figurehead on an ancient sailing vessel, hair streaming behind as she led the way into God knows what. I had been coming to realize that costly decisions loomed before me: whether or not to leave a failed marriage and a job grown stale. Out there between shore and shore, I tried to be still and listen for the voices. I sorted out and fretted and cried a lot. I got very wet. The resolve that began to take shape that afternoon did not come to fruition until several years later, but I know it started in the rain in the bow of that boat. Now and then, it is hard to find one's way. I now needed to come in off the water and reconnect with my community of neighbors.

Neighborhoods and Neighbors

> *In truth, we cannot be fully alive apart from God and neighbor. We ultimately are dependent upon both for identity and nourishment. It may be good and fine to live alone—many of us do. But God never intends for us to live in isolation. We are meant to be together in the neighborhood that is God's realm.*

I have an odd grace in my life: a very poor sense of geographical direction. Friends and family are gleeful witnesses to my deficiency. Colleagues will vouch for the number of times they have repeated routes and landmarks to me, patiently and sometimes even with a straight face. The wonder is that I remain so willing to set out when I have so little idea of what I am doing. But I have called my deficiency a grace on purpose, for without it, I would miss visiting places that are beyond my boundaries. There would be questions I would never think to ask, answers with which I would never have to wrestle, neighborhoods into which I would never set foot.

A case in point: I was leaving Jim's parish at a time of day when negotiating interstate traffic would have been particularly grim, and he suggested an alternate course. The directions went something like this: "Stay on Main Street through College Park; it will become Lee Street, and down around Atlanta University, you will come to Northside Drive, which will take you on back to the cathedral." "Piece of cake," I said and headed off with my usual optimism. Main Street and Lee Street offered no problem. But while I did see friendly landmarks around the edges of the campus complex, Northside Drive never materialized. Then without warning, I was caught in a maze of the bleakest poverty I have encountered anywhere.

The summer's heat had not yet broken, and those seeking relief from whatever lay behind boarded-up windows and shut-fast doors were out in the streets. Very young girls carried half-naked babies on their hips, and young men gathered in clusters around the dark-holed entries to broken-down pool halls and diners. Patches of hard, cracked dirt fronted the dismal houses. I do not remember seeing flowers. At one corner, I drove through water gushing from an open fire hydrant. There was no one playing in its stream. I looked to the left, to the right, to the left again—an aimless and anxious pattern. My hand checked the car's power locks, and my eyes darted to the gas gauge—reflex actions prompted by fear. But in truth, that fear was groundless; no one paid me any mind.

Then just as suddenly as I had entered, I was out. The Georgia Dome loomed before me. I made a quick left turn on the elusive Northside Drive and headed home. Ever since, I have had those streets and those people imprinted on my mind's eye. They continue to come in and out of focus, and they are not pleasant pictures. Even Jim blanched when I told him where I had been. "If you ever go back, you'd better take someone with you." He chuckled, but he was serious. "Why would I ever want to go back?" I reassured myself. I certainly do not belong *there*. It is not my kind of neighborhood.

My husband John and I live in a neighborhood with which I am comfortable. It is located off Old Ivy Road in northeast Atlanta, near the intersection of Piedmont and Roswell Roads, and includes fifty-eight brick townhouses grouped around three interconnected squares—hence the name "Olde Ivy Square." Probably the main things we homeowners have in common are an appreciation of in-town living, gratitude that someone else mows our grass and prunes our bushes, and a certain level of income—we make enough to reside here and do not make enough to be somewhere else. And we supposedly have agreed to abide by the rules of our Olde Ivy Association. These include paying our monthly dues and painting our doors and shutters in standard colors—although strange hues do make their brief appearance from time to time. We take turns serving on the association's policy-setting board, in spite of the fact that we scramble every year to come up with enough people willing to run.

Some of us are retired, while others are young professionals; there are just a couple of children. It is a nice place to live, but on the whole, most of us do not know each other well. The older, original owners are the main exceptions. They have been here for over twenty-five years, and they reminisce about the early days when Olde Ivy was different. The word they use for it is "community," not "neighborhood," referring to something more than an area defined by geographical boundaries. They talk about spontaneous cookouts and about being "real neighbors," pointing back to a day when the residents found time to hobnob and to look after each other. Even now, they quickly organize meals when one of them falls ill or comes home from the hospital. Although I know some people better than others, I still would not use the word "community" to describe us. At the moment, "neighborhood"—that geographical area—works better for me. It says that we are more connected by sidewalks, bylaws, and property values than by relationship, by "neighborliness."

–The Right Answer–

Jesus invites us to look at what in truth, neighborliness *is* with his parable of the Good Samaritan. Luke places it in the middle section of his gospel, often termed the travel narrative because it depicts Jesus' journey to Jerusalem—and to the cross. Luke does not blur the lines of discipleship here but rather lays them down for us clearly and starkly, spelling out the nature of the journey we face as well, as we choose to link our lives with that of Jesus and to travel with him. With this story, we have the opportunity to reexamine what living together as real neighbors might mean.

Along the way to Jerusalem, a cocky lawyer with a question encounters Jesus. He asks, "What must I do to inherit eternal life?" *How do we enter the reign of God?* He wants to test Jesus more than he wants a response. Jesus replies with a question of his own, as he is prone to do: "What is written in the law? You already have the right answer, my friend." The lawyer responds brightly and confidently, knowing that his comeback is correct: "You shall love the Lord your God with all your heart, and with all your soul, and with all you strength, and with all your mind; and your neighbor as yourself." As we listen to the story, we repeat the familiar words with him under our breath, our lips moving along with his. We know the right answer too.

But as I began to learn from my two wise teachers long ago, right answers alone—even complex ones that come out of personal and communal struggle, even ones from the mouth of Jesus—are not enough. If we stop here, pleased with the insights our right answers inspire, we will have stopped short of our destination. There is another question to come—the "so what" question, the one we avoid asking because its answer will present us with a turning point. *What difference will this right answer make in the way we live our lives and make our decisions?* The right answer goes beyond our minds and what they know. It must inflame our hearts, our wills, and our actions.

Jesus goes straight to the essentials with his next words to the lawyer: "Fine. Now do this, and you will live." "Do this?" we ask. "Do what? We have the right creeds, the right formulations. We believe in one God, the Father, the Almighty...Christ has died; Christ is risen...Our Father, who art in heaven...Send us out into the world...I will, with God's help...." We say the words regularly. We say them sincerely. We think we know what they mean, and we pray that the lawyer will stop while he and we are still ahead. But he presses on. "And who is my neighbor?" he asks. Jesus replies with the parable of the good Samaritan.

We know the story—maybe too well. A man is going down from Jerusalem to Jericho on a rocky, steep, and desolate piece of road when a gang attacks him. They strip him of everything he has, beat him savagely, and leave his body on the ground for dead. A priest of the temple comes by and later a Levite, a temple assistant. Both avert their eyes, cross to the other side of the road, and continue on their ways. If we do not grasp the situation, it is easy to cast the two of them in the role of hardhearted heavies, instead of seeing them as men who are simply doing their duty, who are living within the bounds of their faith and minding its rules. They have been set apart for sacred functions, and if either were to touch a dead body, he would be unclean—ritually contaminated and no longer able to carry out his responsibilities in the temple. In this light, they are just obeying the law.

We would be hypocritical if we did not admit that we can identify with these two good law-abiding men. We too try to stay within the bounds of the rules as we understand them—rules of convention if not of religion. We too try to shoulder our responsibilities and to do what is expected of us. We too have set limits and boundaries for ourselves. We have drawn lines over which we will not cross, places we will not go, people we will not greet. We fear we would risk too much if we did—the respect, support, and comfort of our friends, spouses, children, colleagues, those next to us in the pew. We fear we would be left alone, and that would be unbearable. We simply have too much to lose; the cost would be too high.

As Jesus' story goes on, someone does come along for that poor wretch lying beside the road between Jerusalem and Jericho, and he is a Samaritan. To the Jew, he is an outsider, an outcast—someone of the wrong lineage, the wrong background, the wrong religion. But we must approach this part of the parable on tiptoe; we would be hypocrites as well if we jump to identify with him because we know how the story turns out, because we know the Samaritan is the good guy. Rather, he is the one who stands for all those with whom we have difficulty, the ones we would rather did not show up on our doorstep. We might not call them enemies, but in all honesty, we would prefer they go away and leave us alone. Each of us can name a Samaritan or two, and if we are decent, we will squirm as we do.

The Samaritan sees the one in need and stops. He pours oil and wine into the man's wounds and binds them up. He lifts the sagging body onto his ass and carries him to an inn for the night. The next morning, he awakens the innkeeper and gives him two days' compensation and instructions for the care of his patient. "I'm good for the rest on my return," he says. We might say that the Samaritan is foolish. If he is looking for friendship, what he does will probably make no difference—the wounded Jew will still consider him an outcast when all is said and done. The Jew may even die at the inn and waste all that oil and wine. We do not know one way or the other. But the Samaritan does not seem to think he has that much to lose—only some money and maybe a little pride.

Or perhaps a lot more is at stake than appears on the surface. Remember that the lawyer originally asked, "Who is my neighbor?" *Who are my people, my friends, my allies? To whom must I listen? For whom do I bear responsibility? To whom am I obligated?* Jesus tells the parable and then rephrases the lawyer's question, which changes the focus entirely: "Which one of these three, do you think, *was* a neighbor?" *Not obligation, not duty, but relationship.* He is asking what it means to *be* a neighbor. The lawyer once again responds correctly, but this time we can imagine a note of irritation in his voice: "The one who showed mercy." He cannot quite bring himself to say, "the Samaritan," but he has gotten the point. The one who reveals the right answer is the outcast foreigner, the one who gives spontaneously and without self-regard, without weighing penalties or counting cost.

I would suggest that this right answer does not lie in how we define neighbor or neighborhood. It lies instead in whether or not we manage to live in relationship with everyone and everything—regardless of where and with whom we find ourselves. Participation in God's reign is a matter of personal integrity. It has more to do with how we behave toward the stranger on our doorsteps than with the words we recite and the acts of worship we perform. To say we love God, while at the same time turning our backs on those who stand on our thresholds, lie wounded in our streets, or reside in the bleakest sections of our cities, is more than nonsensical—it is impossible.

Life in God's realm is to be like the response of the Samaritan—marked by lavish and abandoned giving even and especially when we think it will make no difference. We are to risk looking foolish, to act as if we have nothing to lose. And here is the paradox, that twist so often found toward the center of God's right answers: *we have everything to lose if we do not.*

Absurd though it may be, we tend to assume that God resides only where we live—physically, intellectually, spiritually. Yet in order to meet God, we all too frequently must take a step away from where we are—a step out of our tidy neighborhoods of comfort. And God is always ready to take us where we have not been, where we may not want to go. God is signaling us to become the persons we have not yet seen ourselves to be. While we are to take heed of the boundaries around us—the laws, rules, and customs of our institutions and our traditions—we need not allow them to capture and enslave us. Again, we must always be asking who or what drew those particular lines in the first place: *Are they of God, or are they not?* We must always judge them according to that rigorous plumb line of God's purposes. We must make the critical distinction between lines that are moral and those that are merely legal—despite whatever personal cost such judgment makes necessary. *When the cost is clear and the promise is vague, watch out; you may be hearing the voice of God!*

Some of the houses I drove by in the Georgia Dome neighborhood may pass the state's building codes—though that taxes my imagination—but for us to allow anyone to live in such miserable surroundings is anything but moral. The lines according to color drawn around water fountains and bathrooms that I remember in the rural South of my childhood were lawful at the time, but they certainly flew in the face of anything we would now describe as just. Legally, to deny anyone the

essentials of daily sustenance, education, or medical bene-
fits is indefensible if we claim that we are all God's children and God loves us equally and we all live in the
neighborhood called God's reign—*the neighborhood God
means to be a community.* The psalmist describes it so ele-
gantly: in this neighborhood "steadfast love and faithfulness will meet; righteousness and peace will kiss each
other. Faithfulness will spring up from the ground, and
righteousness will look down from the sky."

Soon after my escape from those lost streets, I
searched a city map and found their names. They were ordinary ones, like Walnut, Vine, Maple, Elm, and Magnolia, with an Electric Avenue and a Graves Street thrown
in for good measure. I thought that being able to name
the streets would bring the whole experience back into
my world of comfort and familiarity, but it did not work.
In all honesty, I must say that I have no plans to go back
there—and certainly not alone. While my friends and
family may breathe a sigh of relief on hearing such a sensible statement, I do not feel altogether good about making it. To me, God has always seemed to look with favor
and compassion upon those who live outside the boundaries of worldly power and providence—in the shadows of
ancient Jerusalem and the squalor of our Georgia Dome
neighborhoods. And if God is concerned about them,
then I must be too—I am to be their neighbor. Whether
the young lawyer and I like it or not, Jesus would define
neighbor as *anyone* in need.

> For I was hungry and you gave me food, I was thirsty
> and you gave me something to drink, I was a stranger
> and you welcomed me, I was naked and you gave me
> clothing, I was sick and you took care of me, I was in
> prison and you visited me.

But like drawing lines, being a neighbor is not a simple matter. At the risk of letting myself off the hook, I

think there are people better suited than I will ever be to go to Electric Avenue and to serve among the residents of Graves Street. Others have more suitable gifts and graces for such frontline work—talent and training in health care and community organizing, political acumen, and sheer bravado. Even so, my obligation to those people remains—I am their neighbor. So what can I do? I can pay attention to what is going on in my city. I can write letters and make telephone calls to those in positions of power and authority. I can make sure my church is involved. Together, we can provide encouragement and money and supplies to those who do go there; we can offer unceasing prayer. I guess this is another example of drawing lines—lines that distinguish us one from the other, but by distinguishing us also connect us. Still, regardless of the expression of our various gifts, the challenge of the baptized always is to visualize God's neighborhood as bigger and grander than anything we can conceive, without God's help. The responsibility of the baptized is to find ways of distributing all that we have—so everyone and everything can have full share of its abundance.

–Giving and Receiving–

My neighbor Sandra's grandfather understood about sharing. He lived in rural western Tennessee until his death, and well into his nineties he annually planted and tended a large garden. When she asked him why, he responded artlessly, "To share." "With whom?" she protested. "You live alone, and we all live in Atlanta." "Darlin'," he replied in his folksy manner, "with anybody who happens to come along." Every day the old man filled a basket with tomatoes and corn and cucumbers and carried it down to his roadside mailbox. "People comin' by feel free to help themselves, but nobody ever seems to take more than's right. Besides, it's just what the good Lord gives me to start with, and I sure have plenty. Lettin' it rot or eatin' too much would be a sin, now wouldn't it?" Sandra's grandfather had no say in what anyone took or left behind, but it did not matter. To the old man, sharing was just what neighbors did.

Jesus tells a parable about a man who might have appreciated living near Sandra's grandfather. Caught with an unexpected guest in the middle of the night and a bare larder, he needed help from a neighbor. My past experience as a mother of adolescent boys affords me some idea of his predicament.

I was always grateful the boys' friends liked to hang out at our house during those remarkable years. It gave me a measure of assurance that I knew what was going on. What it did not give me was an accurate head count for every meal. The number in the herd grazing through at dinnertime often became a known quantity only as they drew their chairs up to the table. Like every other parent faced with this dilemma on a fairly regular basis, I became adept at extending: another potato or two could add an additional helping to the pot of stew; extra onion and tomatoes could provide another bowl of chili; cheese toast points could take their place in the basket of rolls; meat patties could become thinner... and thinner. But in spite of my ingenuity, there still were those occasions when I could not stretch what I had far enough to go around and I either had to send someone on a quick run to the store or pray that one of the neighbors could come to my rescue.

To understand Jesus' parable, it is helpful to know first of all that travelers often moved at night to avoid the heat of the day. So having a guest show up at midnight might be unexpected but not out of the ordinary. Second, the typical home of the poorer Palestinian consisted of one room with one window. The large family slept close together on mats on a slightly raised platform around the charcoal fire. They were joined for the night by their live-stock—chickens and goats. The entry, open all day long, was then securely barred as the signal they were not to be disturbed. For anyone to get up to answer a knock at the door was to step over and around—or even on—a lot of sleeping bodies and create a great deal of confusion. Jesus, with his marvelous sense of humor, sets the stage for good slapstick comedy. Finally, we must realize that hospitality was a sacred duty, not an optional gesture, if we are to appreciate his story fully. It would not have been enough to extend the stew for the midnight caller: he had to be fed abundantly—with *three* loaves of bread. The embarrassed host does what he has to do. He knocks and knocks at the house next door. His neighbor at last relents, gets up, makes his way through his quota of bodies, and gives the man what he needs. He then goes about quieting down his muttering, whining family and the clucking, bleating animals as he returns to his bed.

Jesus does not say that God wants our frantic pleading. He is saying that when the moment comes, we need to get up and do something. *Ask, and it will be given you; search, and you will find; knock, and the door will be opened for you.* Only then will we be offered God's ready gifts—those gifts we are to distribute freely to our neighbors in God's name. As we look and explore, we will discover the boundlessness of God's realm and the extravagance of God's hospitality. As we present ourselves at the threshold and rap on the door that seems closed, God—our neighbor—will welcome us. Our attitude about giving and receiving only reflects our sense of what God is doing or not doing in our midst. Do we have confidence that God is really acting, and do we believe that God wants us to join in—to be part of the neighborhood?

Jesus calls the man who goes for bread "persistent." The Greek here means "shameless," and it is a critical word to our understanding of the story. We are to be those who persistently knock on the neighbor's door and ask for bread, as well as those who have bread to give when the neighbor appears at ours. We are to be willing to say, "I need you, and I need what you bring to me; I will receive your gifts as I offer you mine in return." Indeed, we may have another definition of being neighbor—and of being hospitable: *the shameless willingness to acknowledge reciprocal need, to reach back and forth with mutual respect across the lines of personal and communal boundary—those semipermeable membranes.* Still, many of us are uncomfortable when we find ourselves on the receiving end—perhaps even with God. We do not want to be obliged to others; we do not want to be in their debt. And we have yet another truth-pointing paradox: *we can only give away what we have first received, and we will be able to receive only as we give away and make room, as we leave empty spaces that can be filled.*

I heard this loud and clear when I first called Bob about coming to the day home, Common Ground, for a conversation with him. He graciously agreed and invited me to stay for lunch with the community. I accepted and manners intact, asked what I could bring. His reply was, "You are the gift. This time, there is nothing else you can bring." They would receive *me* as a gift that day. What a thought! But in giving myself to them—myself unencumbered—I then would be free to receive all they had to offer, and they could be gifts to me as well. It was not going to happen any other way.

–Bread Enough–

And just in case we find ourselves getting nervous about all this giving and receiving among the neighbors in the neighborhood—Will there be enough bread to go around?—Jesus tells the parable of the sower, reminding us of what God is like and offering words of both reassurance and summons. After directing our attention to a nearby field, he begins his story, "Look over there; a sower is walking up and down, scattering his seed to the wind." The grain falls indiscriminately on the path worn by passersby, vulnerable to their trampling feet and to the birds of the air, on the thin layer of soil just covering the rocky limestone shelf beneath, among the buried roots of choking thorns, and on the narrow strips of decent soil. Given how much of it will never amount to anything, we could describe the man as wasteful—profligate and extravagant. Just look at him, walking back and forth in his field, slinging the seed out of the bag he is carrying over his shoulder. He is not paying any mind at all to where it falls. Listen; you can hear him whistling. And how the wind is blowing, carrying the stuff every which way, thither and yon. You'd think he would be more careful. Good seed costs good money, and money doesn't grow on trees—God only knows!

But Jesus is alluding to matters that run counter to our insistence on practical and cost-effective results, our need to crunch numbers and figure it all out. In that open-ended way of the parable, he is inviting us to reflect again on the character of God. He knows that if we do, we may again experience conversion—that whirling around that heads us off in a different direction. While it is true that in God's realm there will be plenty—*is* plenty—in the mystery of things, there will also be loss: death is ever a piece of the graceful cycle of life. But we are not to live in despair. God neither holds back nor allocates stingily. God slings the divine gifts extravagantly out into the wind, knowing the abundant harvest will come. Even so, for now God takes risks: the outcome also depends on us, because God allows us—*wants us*—to have a part. Saying that we are created in God's image means that we are to be extravagant and risk-taking sowers too. We are not to approach life with our arms strapped tightly to our sides.

I once participated in a workshop during which we were invited to recall a teacher who had been particularly important in shaping who we are today. The leader instructed us to write a thank-you letter to that person. I had no trouble coming up with a list. It included my dear grandmother, my parents, some friends, and even my children. In the end, the teacher I selected was that English professor who encouraged me to think for myself. I chose Miss Leyburn because she probably had no idea of her influence on me; she is now dead, so the opportunity to thank her in person has passed—for now anyway. We read our letters out loud, and the reason most of us gave for the choices we made was the same: they did not know; we had never expressed our gratitude. Still, I cannot imagine that many of them expected to be thanked. Rather, they cared about us, and they cared about their relationships and their work, and they finally could not help themselves. They were sowers. They cast their seeds of support and accountability and love into the wind because that is what they were meant to do. And of course, it is what we are meant to do too—to make simple gestures like throwing seed.

I think our call to be extravagant sowers is what is intended in the baptismal promise to proclaim by word and example the Good News of God in Christ—everywhere, to all our neighbors. We are not to care so much about where the seed of our word and deed lands, as we are to be diligent in flinging it forth. We will have little or no idea about the outcome of much that we say and do, and that is probably just as well. Otherwise, we would calculate too finely—think it all through, decide who is deserving and who is not—and we would be too afraid. We would care too much about success. We would want to be effective, make a difference—and that usually gets in the way of being faithful sowers.

At the risk of straining our metaphor a bit too far, I would suggest that we also think of ourselves as seeds, as well as sowers. Not only are we to be sowers of God's good news—encouragement and hope and love—we ourselves are the very ones God casts out into the world. I do not go along with the notion that we are God's hands and feet—God can do quite well without us, thank you, and I cannot help but wonder at times if God would not just as soon go it alone. But God wants our company. God flings us out there to grow into all that we are intended to be. God plants us out there to provide color and shade and food and fresh air for the whole neighborhood. The work is costly—some of us will find ourselves on rocky ground or tossed to and fro by the wind. Few of us will land in decent soil. However, living with such risk is what we do if we are serious about following where Jesus leads—if we are more serious about being faithful sowers than about being successful. Of one thing we can be sure: our best efforts at giving and receiving will not always work out in the ways we anticipate.

Many years ago, I gave a party to which no one came—or rather, they did not come as I had planned. The occasion was New Year's Eve. I was a newly married and hard-up graduate student at Emory University. The party was my culinary debut and a final holiday fling before I resumed the grind and stress of my studies. We compiled our guest list and sent out clever handmade invitations. Envisioning a pleasant and leisurely time with those couples whose company we enjoyed best, we did not invite very many people. Most said yes, and I can still remember the pleasure I received from all the elaborate preparations. I unpacked my wedding-present cookbooks and spent hours poring over their contents, paying little mind to either difficulty or expense. I called my mother and grandmother, requesting recipes for my old favorites from their kitchens. I pulled out every stop I could find, preparing grand molded concoctions and tangy meatballs and hot crab spread. We bought wonderful cheeses and made a terrific—if potent—punch. My *piece de resistance* was a resplendent platter of fruit, glittering with sugar frosting. We cleaned our shotgun duplex as well as its eccentricities allowed, bathed and dressed, stacked records on the turntable, and arranged our feast on every surface we could clear. At eight o'clock in the evening, we pronounced ourselves ready to receive. Our friends came; they nibbled; they left. We had failed to take into account the nature of New Year's Eve and its party-hopping spirit. At midnight, we were four in number, and the remaining food could have fed the masses.

The memory of that New Year's Eve embarrasses me even today. How could I have been so stupid; how could I have called it so poorly? The occasion has come to stand for the place of interior self-doubt that I try to conceal with a carefully draped mantle of confidence. I am afraid that if I voice my ideas, no one will hear. If I write them down, no one will bother to read the words. If I offer a class, few will attend. If I run for office, the vote count will humiliate me. If I apply for the job, someone else will get the call. If I throw a party, the doorbell will remain silent. If I extend a neighborly hand, I will receive a slap. If I sling out my seed, none of it will finally take root and grow. And I suspect I am not alone. So why bother? Why make ourselves so vulnerable and set ourselves up to fail? Why not follow our fears to their ultimate end and give in to self-imposed paralysis? Why not just sit tight and do nothing?

Our answer is, simply, that that is not the way God does things and we are created to be like God. The divine hand is always extended in invitation, and our hands are to be extended as well. The resulting posture looks something like a cross. We might find it less risky not to bother, to leave well enough alone, to mind our own business, to settle for the way things are, but that is not the style of the follower of Jesus. Instead, we are to try again and again, even when we feel foolish in doing so. We are to hang it all out there and throw another party—not worrying about what it will cost or how it will look or what others will say. He promises to be with us when we do. After all, some of our neighbors still live on those bleak streets. Their company might be good.

–Just a Glimpse–

Every once in a while, we get a glimpse of God's neighborhood—even if not yet here in its fullest reality. A woman named Faith owned a townhouse in Olde Ivy Square near ours, but until her last months, we had only a nodding acquaintance between us—generally early in the morning when I was beginning my daily walk and she was exercising her beloved dog Stella. A large and rather formidable woman, Faith was a retired book buyer for a renowned Southern department store. She enjoyed a fine and far-flung reputation among the authors she had known and promoted over the years, but she had now become somewhat of a recluse. I had heard that her living room was furnished literally with stack upon stack of volumes and that her embarrassment over this was the reason most of us had never crossed her front threshold. She seemed like an odd character to me, but I must admit I was curious about what lay behind those closed doors and fastened shutters.

Faith and my husband John had done a stint together on the association board during a time marked by more neighborhood strife than usual. Both eventually had the good sense to resign, and although there was no real disagreement between them, it still took some time before even superficial greetings could be resumed. Unfortunately, many in the neighborhood saw Faith as a negative force; for them, she became the symbol of our discord. She made it her practice to fire off regular letters of complaint to the board and was one of the few confidants of a couple who appeared to delight in sowing seeds of contention.

Then the following June, one of the residents with whom Faith did visit found out she had a rapidly spreading cancer of the pancreas and relayed the news to some of the rest of us. Faith had decided not to undergo the debilitating chemotherapy that at best, would have prolonged her life for a brief time. We had all seen Faith and her dog out together—she even drove Stella around the squares when the weather was too bad for an extended walk! Being animal lovers ourselves, several of us volunteered to take Stella on so that they could enjoy each other's companionship for as long as possible; we knew what the dog's presence would mean to her. Faith reluctantly gave in to us—"I don't want to be an imposition to anyone!"

We dog walkers soon began stopping to talk in the driveway, to comment on the weather and make inquiries about each other's well-being. A healthy grapevine took root, and we made sure everyone stayed up-to-date on Faith's condition when she went into the hospital for several short stays. As for me, more than the dog's short legs were set in motion as I walked her round and round. I saw things in the neighborhood I had not previously noticed: flowers planted and doors freshly painted and burned-out porch lights. I had conversations with people who until now had been only names on the printed roster. I took pleasure in leaving bags of cucumbers and peppers from our over-active garden hanging on doorknobs. In short, the place became my home—a real neighborhood—more than ever before.

After a while, Faith began inviting me and others to come in when we came by to pick up and deliver the dog and to run the small errands she allowed. We all crossed paths in the back room that served as her living space—the stacks of books in the front room had not been exaggerated. I enjoyed my brief times with her, learning a little of her history and telling her bits of my own. Among other things, I discovered that her name was—is—Mary Faith. A lapsed Methodist who had claimed to be something of an agnostic in these last years, she now asked John to bring communion and anoint her before one of her stays in the hospital. He did, and the visit was not his last. He and Faith talked about books they enjoyed and people they knew, and John managed to slip in some theology about healing. He explained that it constituted a change of attitude toward a disease, as distinguished from its elimination, a cure. She seemed to understand.

In late August, Faith decided she would like to have a few members of the neighborhood join in a service of healing in her home. She composed her list, and I made the telephone calls. Several seemed surprised to be invited, but everyone came—including the seed-sowing couple. Counting John and Mary Faith, there were ten of us that Saturday morning—Stella made it eleven. We all laid hands on Faith and on each other; we exchanged the kiss of peace and received communion. One of the women gave her a small amber cross she had brought home from Russia, and John blessed it. Word of the service spread through the neighborhood, and the spirit of the event took hold even among those who had not been there. I heard reports of notes written and apologies extended. We received a few ourselves. Shortly afterward, Faith asked John to come over to talk and pray. Her condition was deteriorating, and she knew it. Still, she spoke of her healing. That evening John administered the last rites of the church to our cantankerous and game friend—our neighbor—who by the way, fired off letters to the board until the very end. She died the next week.

Many in the neighborhood attended the September service at a local funeral home large enough to hold the crowd. The officiant was the pastor of the little Methodist church around the corner where she had transferred her membership—typically Faith, by telephone. With humor and poignant jabs, the eulogist did a masterful job of portraying the rich character of his unforgettable friend—and ours. He even pronounced a directive on her behalf: the contentious couple would be denied their request to adopt Stella. *They will not have my dog! They have four cats, and Stella hates cats!* We listened to her favorite poems and sang "Amazing Grace." How Mary Faith must have loved the whole thing.

I am not sure she would have any use for words like "repentance" and "forgiveness" and "reconciliation" to express what had taken root among all of us, but I do not know any other way to talk about it. If repentance means turning around and seeing things in a different way, I think that is what she was about in her last days—still remaining the same old obstreperous Faith. I think that is what she was acknowledging when she talked about being healed. I never told her—she would have hooted—but her story recalls for me the one about the prodigal son. Like that younger boy, Faith seemed to come to her senses and head home. She seemed to repent and forgive, and we did some of the same. Reconciliation—literally, bringing together again—began. Strained relationships in her own family were eased, and things were better between her and members of our neighborhood. After all, she had opened the door of her home and allowed some of us to pass over the threshold, to come inside. Once again, the word for this is "hospitality," welcoming an enemy as guest—being neighbor.

Maybe reconciliation is another definition for the boundary crossing that occurs when we turn around and let go, when we step over and out of the dividing compartments into which we have boxed ourselves and others—those premature coffins. Faith took us as far as she could, right up to her final earthly threshold. And what did she do? She threw a party—two of them if you count the healing service and the amazing-grace funeral.

I have to confess things are not that different in Olde Ivy Square these days. We are pretty much back to being a geographic neighborhood more than a real community. A number of new residents have moved in, and once again, we do not know each other very well. It appears to me that the level of petty bickering—or indifference—has risen. Still, some of us did have that glimpse of new possibility, and it would be a shame to lose sight of it. In the neighborhood of God, you see, everything is new and fresh and rich with color and possibility. As Paul writes to the Ephesians, in Christ Jesus the rigid walls of division and hostility between us are broken down. We are no longer strangers and aliens to each other—we are neighbors. We call out words of greeting and welcome across our boundaries. Doors stand open, and thresholds are crowded.

Good Fences

I have long loved the poetry of Robert Frost, who paid annual visits to my college, Agnes Scott. I was a senior the year before he died, and I had the honor of introducing him to the reverent assembly of students and faculty. Among my favorites of his poems is "Mending Wall." I come across it often in a treasured little book he signed for me. The spidery handwriting gives testimony to his age at the time, but it belies the power of his reading that night and the ongoing strength of his work today. In "Mending Wall," Frost speaks of two New England neighbors who every spring, walk the line—the boundary—separating their adjoining properties to inspect and repair a rock wall damaged by the ravages of winter. The narrator begins:

> Something there is that doesn't love a wall,
> That sends the frozen-ground-swell under it,
> And spills the upper boulders in the sun;
> And makes gaps even two can pass abreast.

His companion simply says, "Good fences make good neighbors," and the poem continues with the first man's response:

Spring is the mischief in me, and I wonder
If I could put a notion in his head:
"Why do they make good neighbors? Isn't it
Where there are cows? But here there are no cows.
Before I built a wall I'd ask to know
What I was walling in or walling out,
And to whom I was like to give offence.
Something there is that doesn't love a wall,
That wants it down."

The last line is his neighbor's reply:

He says again, "Good fences make good neighbors."

We might note that repairing the wall does bring the two men together at least once a year, and so it paradoxically serves both to separate and connect them.

Frost's two neighbors do not merely raise the question of whether or not we need fences—boundaries. To that query—joining the second voice in the poem—I can easily answer yes. Without good and solid boundaries and the identity, definition, and protection they afford us, we would not be able to be in relationship with each other in ways we would also consider good. *Good fences make good neighbors.* But then, the narrator's musings about this claim go on to underscore my awareness that a boundary is more complex than it often appears to be on the surface—as we have said throughout the pages of this book. *Before I built a wall I'd ask to know....* Indeed, the interchange between the two men sets me wondering all over again about concerns like, when should we build a wall or a fence in the first place—and when should we tear one down? Should we invite anyone to help us or do we go it alone? Their words summon me to consider once more what it means to be a neighbor. They take me right back to where we began—to that essential but

irresolvable tension between boundary and hospitality—and I remember the wise man's saying about cost
and promise.

—Another Fence—

Another story about a fence keeps the same questions
spinning around in my head. A church I have known for a
number of years is an old and proud one. Neo-Gothic in
design, its soaring, stained-glass windows both depict
scenes from the life of Jesus and tell birth-to-death narra-
tives of the distinguished families who gave them. The
brick façade, with its heavy, red wooden doors, sits close
to the sidewalk of a major street in the midst of one of our
large cities. Various wings and stories have been added
onto the original structure over time; several annexed
buildings complete the sprawling complex.

For a long while, the public identity of this church has
been that of a sanctuary for literally hundreds of homeless citizens. Staff and volunteers have furnished medical
and job-training assistance. A post office has given them
a place to receive mail and thus maintain some measure of
connection with their families, while providing that personal address so essential to the successful landing of a
job. A Friday service of worship has invited those lining
up for the daily lunch into a community of prayer. Even
so, as members of the congregation began realizing that
most of the men and women who came by on a regular basis had been doing so for years, they started wondering
whether or not they were meeting such overwhelming
needs in the most responsible and effective of ways. Were
they giving their guests a substantial leg up out of the
seemingly bottomless pit into which they had fallen, or
were they just offering temporary relief—salve and
Band-Aids?

Then, to complicate matters all the more, concerns about the cost being paid by the church itself started to mount. That many people cannot regularly stream through a facility without its taking a beating, and the look of the building went from suitably shabby to embarrassingly run-down. The parish hall, with its ever-present smell of urine, was less and less a popular choice for wedding receptions and parish gatherings. In addition, incidents of theft and vandalism were on the rise. The disappearance of an altar cross was the final straw, and for the first time in remembered congregational history, its leadership made the reluctant decision to lock those red front doors. No longer would the nave's pews supply beds for those without anywhere left to go. As a consequence, the front yard and steps were increasingly used as public bathrooms, replete with foul messages scrawled on the walkways. Members loudly voiced their outrage: "It's no wonder we have difficulty attracting younger families here. Who would want their kids to step in excrement on their way to Sunday school—or to pick up a needle or a condom?" And, "These people think they own the streets! Aren't we doing everything we can? This is a fine way to show their thanks!" The inevitable talk of building a fence soon began, and it immediately raised all sorts of boundary questions for the congregation.

True, the fence would be a physical line providing defense against further defacing of the church's property. Parents could once again allow their children free run of the front yard without worrying about what they might land on or come across, and drug traffickers would not have such easy access to the students attending a street academy housed in one of the annexes. The fence also would give needed aesthetic definition to the rambling church plant, unifying the various buildings; a truly handsome one could even be an artistic contribution to the surrounding cityscape. Nevertheless, members still had to deal with the guilt and ambivalence that kept popping up in their deliberations: "Aren't we just doing a lot of rationalizing in our own self-interest?" "Sure, the fence would protect us, and maybe it could be made to look good. But wouldn't it tell the rest of the city that we no longer welcome those lines of souls at our doors?" "Wouldn't we become just another mighty brick fortress? That's not what we've stood for all these years!" So the arduous struggle went on.

I am not sure exactly what turned the tide. The nature of the struggle itself probably made the difference—the fact that the leaders created an atmosphere of safety and openness and permitted an honest discussion of difficult questions among the whole congregation. In the course of these deliberations, they came to realize that they were not willing to communicate the message "anything goes." They saw this as both irresponsible and inaccurate; in truth, they would not tolerate anything and everything under the guise of caring. That, they concluded, is not caring in the end. To care is to set limits and expectations, not to check out in apathy or with cold feet. So for the present in any case, they chose not to provide a facility that would be open twenty-four hours a day. And they decided that building a fence would be a good thing for them to do: it would help them define who they are and declare that identity to others. Further, they determined that the fence did not necessarily have to establish whether or not they were an open community. That had to happen—or not—in other ways.

The black wrought-iron fence is up. Its firm line of spiky points is broken along the way by wide-swinging gates. A local ordinance says that the better-looking side must be turned outward to face the public. I guess it is; I really cannot see much difference between the two. While the front gates are kept locked except when security guards are on duty for scheduled events, the complex is generally accessible during business hours—you only have to know where the side entrances are located. Predictably, there are those who think the fence is quite handsome and others who are horrified—including past members of the church who have moved away. To them, it screams, "Unwelcome!" They fear that with the building of the fence, the church has loosened its grasp on a spirit of hospitality to the suffering poor and is in danger of losing its heart and soul. Still, regardless of all the responses and opinions, the parish's various services to the homeless go on, continuing to evolve and expand—now in more thoughtful cooperation with other inner-city churches rather than in isolation. I would say that for the present time, a number of people remain somewhat ambivalent about the decision to build the fence, unsure of its ultimate cost. Their answer to the question of whether good fences in fact make good and responsible neighbors must come in future days.

--Cost--

There is some price to pay with virtually every decision we make, every line we draw, and we are probably fortunate in not always knowing what it will be. Otherwise, we might too often choose to do nothing, to stay put with the status quo. When Bartimaeus, the blind beggar, decides to call out to Jesus, the prospect of cost is likely the furthest thing from his mind. His custom has been to sit by the side of the Jericho to Jerusalem road, shaking the coins already dropped into his cup, signaling for more to be added. This is how he has made his living all these years—such as it is—and he has come to a measure of peace with his lot in life. Today, the roadside crowd is larger than usual. The annual Passover pilgrimage to Jerusalem is underway, and Bartimaeus rattles his cup with greater vigor than usual. The name "Jesus" is on every tongue around him as the young Galilean rabbi and his entourage move along the way. Bartimaeus has heard that the man is a healer, and his internal kaleidoscope now takes a wild spin. A whole new hope comes into focus—right before his useless eyes. He sees that Jesus holds for him the promise of sight, and he cries out again and again, "Jesus, Son of David, have mercy on me!" The crowd tries to shut him up, but with every rebuke, he just shouts all the louder. To everyone's surprise, Jesus stops in his tracks. He says, "I see him; bring him here." Bartimaeus leaps to his feet and flings aside his cloak, the fickle crowd moving him forward. Jesus asks a single question, "What do you want me to do for you?" Bartimaeus simply answers, "I want to see." And Jesus says, "Go; your faith has made you well."

There is not much doubt about Bartimaeus' future had he not decided to call out to Jesus: he would have ended his days by the side of the road, begging for coins. Still, we might wonder what happened after he gained his sight. At the end of the gospel narrative, it has not yet dawned on him that there will be some cost to his healing; that realization is yet to come. He will have to give up his cup and his familiar place by the side of the road. No one wants to throw coins to an able-bodied, sighted man. He will have to go to work and take up a life altogether different from the one he has led. Although the implied ending to the story has him flinging away the cup and stepping out into a life of new promise, the truth is that we really do not know what befalls Bartimaeus. Perhaps he finally cannot square himself with his change in fortune. Perhaps he comes to regret his calling out to Jesus for healing and wishes he had just left things alone. Deciding to make a change—to be hospitable to a new possibility—is never a simple matter.

Bartimaeus' blindness was not voluntary. His choice lay in doing something about it—at whatever the unforeseen cost. While my son's choice of employment was his own, he too decided he had to make a change—at considerable cost. Jonathan called to tell me that he was quitting his job. He really could not afford to do so, since he was in between two graduate degrees in botany and needed to save money. But he explained that he was having difficulty looking at himself in the mirror these days. Jonathan was working as an "environmental consultant." He took the job believing that he would be assisting companies in finding ways to preserve natural resources. Instead, he found his job was to look for loopholes in regulations and help companies find marginally legal—and to him, immoral—ways of wriggling around existing safeguards. The name "environmental consultant" did not fit what he indeed was doing, and he found the courage to give his work a more accurate one—something like "industry consultant." As we have previously said, a name or title is part of what constitutes a boundary and gives form to us as persons and communities. In searching for the right name, Jonathan was dealing with matters of his own identity and integrity, and the revised name was not one with which he could live. Fortunately, he soon found another job in his field—but at less than half the salary. The long-term cost to him was that his student loans would be larger and would take longer to pay off. He learned that there is a price to principle. However—this time anyway—he decided it was worth paying.

My son's decision also raised all sorts of uncomfortable questions for me, questions with which I must continue to wrestle if I am to call things by their right names, if I am to struggle with that tension between boundary and hospitality—between standing for something and being open to new understandings and new ways:

- What comes within the bounds of our present legal system but falls outside the moral bounds of God's neighborhood?

- What is my response to: "It's okay; everybody's doing it"?

- Is it ever all right to tell a lie—even a so-called white lie?

- Is it ever all right to steal—even if my family is hungry?

- Am I ever justified in taking a life—even in self-defense, even in the face of great wrong?

- How much help can I be expected to give—within the bounds of my own limitations, my fences?

- When and for what would I be willing to go to jail?

- How far will I go before I draw my lines—about where I live, where I work, what and how much I buy, to what I can belong?

- Where would Jesus draw his lines?

Jesus has more of his difficult words for us about the cost of following in his way and deciding to become part of the neighborhood of God. He speaks of those hard roads and narrow doors, of taking up crosses and facing persecution in his name. I know there are Christians then and now who can give firsthand testimony to the truth of his words, but if I am honest, I must admit that they do not match my experience. I have never been persecuted for my membership in the church; it has never been a disadvantage for me. Oh, there may be some who call me crazy when I head out on a cold and drizzly Sunday morning, but that is about it. My identification with the church is more like a badge of good citizenship. Indeed, many of my convictions—particularly those regarding matters of social justice—are attributed to my politics rather than to my faith. I share them with many who do not affiliate with any religious body.

But to paraphrase a saying I remember from the sixties, not to decide is to make a decision as well—with its own subsequent cost—and I wonder if we good church people have looked closely enough at ourselves and been willing to make those hard decisions that keep us true to our identity as followers of Jesus. Maybe we have no inside that in fact differs significantly from what lies outside our boundaries. Maybe our boundaries are too flimsy and too porous—not good fences. Maybe the world simply dismisses us as inconsequential and irrelevant. Maybe we are too bland to incur its hostility. Maybe we have sold out for too much comfort and favor to warrant a great deal of notice at all. Maybe we are just not enough like Christ to be persecuted in this name. A lower-church friend has said of incense, "Can't do any harm; can't do any good." Maybe this applies to us who say we are ministers of good news: Can't do any harm; can't do any good. I think it is time we ask ourselves the question about everything we are and everything we do: *What does this have to do with the reign of God?* The cost of our choosing not to ask and answer that question can be the forfeiture of everything God promises for us, and our separation from God's bountiful neighborhood of peace and justice.

–Promise–

Over twenty years ago, my husband John had one of those glimpses into the neighborhood. He had been invited to Northern Ireland to lead a conference for six Roman Catholic priests and six Protestant pastors, sponsored by the community of Corrymeela—Hill of Harmony. The community was formed by a small group of Protestants and Catholics who covenanted to live together in the town of Ballycastle near Belfast until peace came to their country. It is still there today. John chose baptism—the line encircling us as Christians and making us one body in Christ—as the theme of the conference. However, as it unfolded, things were not going well. The two parties were becoming more and more entrenched in their positions and alienated from each other. The atmosphere of the early morning gatherings for Bible study and silent prayer became increasingly icy as the week progressed. Participants sat stiffly and silently around the edge of the room, separated into their respective camps. Protestant and Catholic children who were attending their own event sat in the middle of the floor—probably not sure whether they should speak to each other or not.

Then on the fifth day, two people crossed a boundary and met on common ground. John had told the story of the woman who touched the fringe of Jesus' cloak and was healed. As the group continued in silence, an old Franciscan priest in his long, brown robe broke rank with the other adults and slipped to the floor among the children. A little girl leaned over to him and whispered, "May I touch you?" "Certainly," he whispered back. "I'm scared," she confessed. "Why?" he asked. "Because if my father knew, he would beat me." "Maybe he doesn't need to know." The child reached forward, patted the fabric of his sleeve, and cautiously touched his hand with her index finger. Abruptly pulling back, she looked at it and said, "Nothing happened." "Oh, yes it did," her accomplice responded. "After today, you and I will never again see the world as we have before." And the ice in the room cracked open, releasing the waters of renewal. Before heading home, the priests and pastors embraced in a fresh commitment to their mutual quest for peace.

God comments on the scene through the voice of the prophet Isaiah:

Do not remember the former things, or consider the things of old. I am about to do a new thing; now it springs forth, do you not perceive it? I will make a way in the wilderness and rivers in the desert. The wild animals will honor me, the jackals and the ostriches; for I give water in the wilderness, rivers in the desert, to give drink to my chosen people, the people whom I formed for myself so that they might declare my praise.

Robert Grosseteste, bishop of Lincoln in the thirteenth century, says it like this: "Every new thing which implants and promotes and perfects the new man, corrupts and destroys the old. Blessed is the new, and in every way welcome to him who comes to recreate the old man in newness." Alienation and death are the end if we persist in doggedly hanging on to the old ways. Life is the end if we are willing to turn around and let go—to risk being the empty tombs we become in baptism.

Still, venturing to reach out and touch the robe of the "enemy"—like the little girl did—is not something I do without thinking twice and taking several deep breaths and maybe even closing my eyes. I am afraid of what doing so will mean for me. I wonder if I will be up to the challenge. And I have a hard time remembering that God does seem to delight in inviting ordinary and flawed human beings to do extraordinary things—to be extraordinary and cherished residents of the holy neighborhood. Time and again, I have to pull out Paul's words of deliverance in his letter to the Romans, telling me that I no longer need be trapped in the old bondage of sin and death and nerveless fear:

> No, in all these things we are more than conquerors through him who loved us. For I am convinced that neither death, nor life, nor angels, nor rulers, nor

things present, nor things to come, nor powers, nor
height, nor depth, nor anything else in all creation,
will be able to separate us from the love of God in
Christ Jesus our Lord.

What a statement! Nothing and nobody in any way, at
any time, in any place can usher us out of God's neighborhood—unless we ourselves choose not to live within its
borders. That is God's promise.

With the life, death, and resurrection of Jesus Christ,
God marks a boundary that is intended to include all of
humanity and the entire creation. For me, the Great Vigil
of Easter celebrates this reality as does no other Christian
liturgy, and for this reason, it has become my favorite of
the church year. I love the drama of it, the building of ex-
citement as we conclude our annual trek through Holy
Week and gather around the fire to tell the ancient stories of God's saving presence among us.

One particular Easter Vigil stands out in my memory.
During the preceding days, the shadows of the valley of
death had seemed darker than ever, as I was deluged with
news of sickness and death. The annual unfolding of the
familiar Holy Week services only served to reinforce my
downhearted spirit. But Sunday finally came, and I rolled
out of bed into the dark morning and made my way to the
church garden for the lighting of the vigil fire. From it,
we kindled the paschal candle and then the candles each
of us held. The shadows began to back off. I fell into the
line of the procession and gingerly entered the dark
church, running my fingers over the smooth wood of the
pews to guide myself along. We moved forward to the
bell-clear tones of the cantor chanting the haunting Ex-
sultet, and we sat in candlelight as the old stories were
read anew. And just as we burst into the Gloria, the shadows evaporated, and the light of day streamed in around
us. We could not have stopped it if we had wanted to.

We baptized seven souls into our company on that Easter morning. They were drowned in the waters of Christ's death—submerged in the shadows of the valley—and they were lifted up into the life of fire and story, water and spirit, bread and wine. We welcomed them into the new neighborhood and assured them that the word indeed is good. They, like us, will have to decide whether or not they will stay—whether they will struggle with boundary and hospitality, with cost and promise. We must not forget to pass on to them the wise man's counsel: *When the cost is clear and the promise is vague, watch out. You may be hearing the voice of God!*

Questions for Discussion

PROLOGUE
Lines

1. What lines can you recall from your own childhood story that were particularly important in shaping who you are today?

2. Are there lines you encounter today that are especially confusing or frustrating, reassuring or comforting to you? Why do you experience them in this manner?

3. What lines might God be now drawing or erasing in our midst as a church community? What is your evidence for these changes? How do you feel about them?

ONE
Inside and Outside

1. What are the boundaries you have inherited and have set yourself that establish your personal identity?

2. What boundaries have you experienced in the church that help you to understand your identity as a baptized person?

3. When have you crossed a boundary you set for yourself? What was that experience like? How did you feel? How have you changed as a result?

4. What boundaries and/or lack of boundaries that others have set for themselves make you feel secure? Insecure?

TWO
Welcome

1. How have you experienced the difference between being welcomed and being included?

2. What or who are the enemies you need to welcome? What would it look like if you did? What would change?

3. When have you experienced hospitality most fully?

4. What experience has made you feel most unwelcome? How did you react? What did you learn from your reaction?

THREE
Connections

1. When have you experienced the breaking of one of your boundaries that worked against a relationship?

2. How can you reveal love for someone by establishing your own boundaries for the relationship?

3. When have you established a boundary in order to connect with someone while maintaining your identity?

4. When has a confrontation about differences in boundaries resulted in a healthier, stronger relationship?

FOUR
Closed and Open

1. When have you experienced boundaries that were too rigid? Too loose? What effect did those boundaries have in your life?

2. What boundaries in your life are you least likely to open? Why?

3. When have you risked crossing a boundary? What helped you find the courage to take that risk?

4. When have you chosen not to risk crossing a boundary? Why did you make that choice?

5. When have you had a good experience in being flexible about boundaries? A bad experience?

FIVE
Moving and Changing

1. What are some of the reasons that might justify changing a boundary?

2. Have your boundaries changed over the years? How? Why?

3. When have you been most happy or sad as a consequence of changing or not changing a boundary?

4. When has your congregation experienced moving into a new or out of an old boundary? What motivated the change?

SIX
Neighborhoods and Neighbors

1. What does the neighborhood of God look like to you? Tell of a time when you experienced some dimension of that neighborhood.

2. In your experience, what has being a good neighbor to do with boundaries and hospitality?

3. When have you been neighbor to someone? When has someone been neighbor to you?

4. In your experience, when has it been difficult to be a good neighbor? Where are you now being called to move forward and be a good neighbor or contribute to a healthy neighborhood?

EPILOGUE
Good Fences

1. When have you or your congregation had to consider the cost and the promise of either keeping or changing a boundary?

2. What criteria did you use when deciding which way to go?

3. When have you experienced God's spirit calling you out of the familiar and safe to risk a change in belief, attitude, or behavior?

4. What are the most important insights and the most compelling or troublesome implications you have experienced in reflecting on this book?